"*Pilgrimage* is a searingly h̶c̶ journey from an outwardly successful [radiol...] physician with little time for serious self-reflection to a professional guide with a God-centered program for promoting emotional and physical well-being. Although the book delves deeply into her first emotionally traumatic marriage and the challenges of practicing cancer and primary care medicine in the broken U.S. healthcare system, ultimately the wounds that Dr. Chacko is most concerned about healing are those of the mind and spirit. Readers will come away from *Pilgrimage* with a broader understanding of health, the power of prayer, and the many paths toward personal and spiritual fulfillment."

—**Kenny Lin**, physician; deputy editor, *American Family Physician*; professor of clinical family medicine, Georgetown University School of Medicine

"I had the privilege of living in community with Donna—working and worshipping with her—and saw how her love and compassion fostered healing. In this extraordinary memoir, Donna describes the pain, sorrow, loss, and hope she experienced as she tried to understand who she is, to whom she belongs, and where she is going. Her words are a witness to all of us, as she encourages us to make our own journey, with God at our side, to new happiness, peace, and life."

—**Janelle Goetcheus**, physician; cofounder, Christ House, Washington, DC

"*Pilgrimage* is an honest and soulful depiction of real life, the struggles of an often emotionally challenging career, complicated relationships, and competing demands. As a physician Dr. Chacko demonstrates a natural propensity to witness and work through the pain of others while denying her own. She gently opens her heart and our eyes to the healing power of self-reflection, prayer, and self-care. Her journey demonstrates the beauty of discovering the presence and power of God in the midst of a life of service and sacrifice."

—**Lisa Banks-Williams**, psychiatric nurse practitioner; adjunct assistant professor, Georgetown University School of Nursing and Health Studies; and pastor

"By revisiting and reinterpreting her own life, Dr. Chacko has done a great favor for us all. She helps us see how we are wounded by unhuman expectations, the hurt humanity of our relatives and friends, and modern life in the world—out there in the nothingness of comfort and lack of commitment. Reading *Pilgrimage* will help you regain an interior life, heal your soul, and find your own path to the great healer, Jesus himself."

—**Fr. Roberto J. Cortes-Campos**, pastor, St. Mark the Evangelist Catholic Church, Hyattsville, MD

"This is the story of an accomplished doctor and her family—a family of accomplishment, means, and stature, the kind I often call a 'looking good family.' It has been my experience that members of these families often have difficulty validating their pain and difficulties, a vital component of healing, because of their privilege and outward-appearing lack of dysfunction. Dr. Chacko generously pulls back the curtain to let us know all is not always what it seems. In so doing her story will help others overcome shame and see what is possible.

I highly recommend this book to anybody who has felt hopeless and needs an identifiable and compassionate roadmap, along with good company, to a life with more freedom and more connection to Love, the Energetic Source behind all life, whom many call God."

—**Marilyn Williams**, psychotherapist

"Dr. Donna Chacko begins her book with a simple yet profound goal: to offer hope to all who struggle with life's many challenges. And her book does just that. By drawing on her professional experience, family story, and faith, Dr. Chacko offers a compelling path to wholeness of body, mind, and spirit that all seek on the pilgrimage of life."

—**Jem Sullivan**, educator and author of five books on faith formation

"Poignant and redemptive, Donna's story is a well-crafted reminder that God is intimately involved in even the worst parts of our lives. And God is more invested in our happy ending than we ever imagined."

—**Chad R. Allen**, entrepreneur and consultant

"Dr. Chacko endured a challenged marriage and a demanding role in her medical field. What adversity taught her was to be even more concerned about the poor and underserved. Her ministry, Serenity and Health, is now the fruit of her labor. If a memoir is to inspire, consider this book your next read."

—**Sister Mary Margaret Funk**, Benedictine nun and author

"I found every paragraph captivating, urging me to go to the next paragraph, the next page, the next section. I was, and still am, totally

invested in Donna's story. The book's layout, writing style, and easy flowing prose drew me in to the point of not realizing time was passing. The evolution of Donna's story is honest and fair, and I think it will resonate with everyone who has ever been in a relationship, raised a family, or struggled with balancing family and career."
—**Caryn Tilton,** management consultant

"Donna's memoir is a captivating story of how God's ever-present grace guided her through the peaks and valleys of life. This book is a treasure trove filled with hope, inspiration, and practical tools to integrate one's mind, body, and spirit."
—**Brian J. Plachta**, author, spiritual director, and attorney

"Donna Chacko's courageous self-examination of her trials and triumphs is a prescription for finding a figurative lump in the heart and how to heal such a wound. Her inside-out journey to wholehearted living x-rays the emotional pain of relationships with an eye trained for unhealthy growth and a heart filled with regret. Her memoir spans painful physical disability, PTSD, dark cognitive dissonance, and graced healing through the Divine Therapist. What a delight to discover in the final chapters a changed tone of voice, a compassionate heart, and helpful resources from her ever-present desire to heal."
—**Chris Manion**, award-winning author

"We humans are fragile and flawed, aren't we? Despite seemingly bounteous blessings, we lose sight of purpose and passion in the trappings of our false selves. The road to self-awareness and acceptance is fraught with bumps and detours. By sharing her own story of wayfinding, Dr. Chacko provides us with a compelling reason and roadmap to carry on."
—**Peggy Winton**, CEO, Association for Intelligent Information Management

"Donna was my best friend in high school. She became a physician and I became a high school math teacher. In this compelling telling of her journey, she proves to be the ultimate teacher between the two of us. She provides a crystal-clear view of struggles we rarely imagine a successful professional, mother, and role model would experience. She then masterfully teaches the reader specific tools that can be applied in their own walk through life."
—**Margo Lee Bellock**, retired high school math teacher and principal

PILGRIMAGE:
A DOCTOR'S HEALING JOURNEY

Pilgrimage

A Doctor's Healing Journey

DONNA CHACKO, MD

LUMINARE PRESS
WWW.LUMINAREPRESS.COM

Luminare Press
442 Charnelton St.
Eugene, OR 97401
www.luminarepress.com

LCCN: 2021909099
ISBN: 978-1-64388-652-7

To my family—
and yours

Contents

Preface

Decades practicing medicine and years agonizing in my marriage taught me truths about health I never learned in medical school. I'm eager to share everything I learned because I'm convinced it can transform your life, as it transformed mine.

The stakes are high. As a physician and since retiring I have witnessed growing levels of anxiety, depression, chronic illness, obesity, and addiction. I've seen hurting families and marriages, declining participation in churches and community organizations, and growing unease about the state of our world. As I write this, the historic COVID-19 pandemic and the raw fissures in our society and politics have created a level of stress we couldn't have imagined a few years ago.

But I want you to know something up front: there is hope. Imagine yourself standing tall and smiling as you start each day. You are grateful to know your purpose in life, and you face the day with enthusiasm, energy, and peace of mind. You seize the day to joyfully serve God and others and to move toward your goals with regard to family, work, or self-care. This may seem out of reach right now, but it is absolutely possible for you.

How do I know? I've learned from many teachers, starting with my patients. They showed me how health can be enhanced by interactions of mind, body, and spirit. For twenty years I practiced radiation oncology and saw how my patients' faith, love of family, and purpose in life kept them strong. I remember being awed, for example, by the profound peace and strength demonstrated by a tiny, wrinkled older woman with painful terminal cancer. As she spoke lovingly of her Lord, her body visibly softened at the relief she found in his presence.

At the age of fifty-one, I retrained in family medicine and then worked in Washington, DC, in a clinic for the poor and immigrants, and in Christ House, a medical recovery facility for the homeless. I saw how stress and trauma create physical and mental illness—I also saw how faith, love, respect, listening, and community promote healing.

One teacher was Joe, a sick, silent, bent-over homeless man. He clutched his black plastic garbage bag stuffed with his belongings as he shuffled down the hall after being admitted to Christ House. He was slowly brought back to life by the tender care and love he received. As his long-buried hope came alive, he started talking, laughing, and healing.

Another teacher was a new immigrant named Maria. She returned over and over to the clinic with headaches, insomnia, back pain, and depression. Nothing seemed to help until she enrolled in the English-language school, got a part-time job, and made friends. Soon all of her ailments resolved.

My long and difficult marriage was my most challenging teacher—it took a long time for me to grasp the lessons. Despair drove me to the edge of a dark pit, where I finally turned to God. Over time I made a project of understanding who I was, what motivated me, and the source of healing. My anguish as a wife and mother helped me appreciate how human suffering is so much more than a disease or diagnosis that can be treated with a pill or a medical procedure, and how health means so much more than the absence of disease.

The remarkable truth is that abundant health, or being fully alive in body, mind, and spirit, is available to all of us, even during illness or adversity. My life experiences have demonstrated that this kind of whole health is rooted in faith (for me, a deep trust in Jesus) and requires intentional self-care of both body and mind, as well as traditional health care.

I sincerely believe that my story and the stories of others you'll meet in these pages, along with the steps I describe, can help you find your own path to more abundant health. You can thrive even during our challenging times.

The time to begin is now.

I pray that God will bless you on your journey.

PART I

The Pit

1

Confrontation

I finally did it. I informed my husband that I was taking our three daughters to visit my twin brother, Danny, in New Mexico. I hadn't seen my brother for several years and wanted the girls to get to know their cousins.

I had done all the research about dates, flights, and arrangements to cover my absence from my medical practice. I tried to explain to Jacob, my husband, how important this trip was for me and encouraged him to come along, prattling: "They want you to come. They have plenty of space. New Mexico is so beautiful." He was not interested. I continued to offer up the details, potential dates, and my views about how good it would be for our girls to know their cousins. He just wouldn't talk about it. I recognized his fears about the risk of flying, particularly with the children, but he wouldn't talk about these worries. So, I just discounted his concerns as inflated and ignored them.

I always went along with him on big things. Flying from Florida to New Mexico with our school-age daughters was definitely a big thing. But this time was different. I had made up my mind. I had a reasonable plan, and I was going.

I braced myself and quickly bought the airline tickets. I was nervous—actually, I was scared. What would happen? I searched for hints from him, but there were none.

The intervening weeks before the departure date passed with near silence between us. Each night we went to bed in our master bedroom suite on the second floor of our grand home, lying as far apart as we could in our king-size bed. The script was far different from the "happily ever-after" story I'd hoped for when we moved into our dream house the previous year.

In the days leading up to the planned trip, I pretended all was OK. It's weird to think a hidden video of an evening with our family would have looked and sounded nearly normal. At dinner the five of us would all be sitting together in our breakfast nook chatting and laughing about the day. There was a wall between him and me that I pretended wasn't there. I smiled as normally as I could while stuffing the pain deep into my chest. I wonder what the girls must have thought as we acted out this tragic play.

The morning of our planned departure is scarred into my memory. The girls and I gathered our packed bags and paused in the vaulted foyer to say good-bye to Dad. As we moved to the door, he blocked our way. I froze and, while staring at his stony face, saw his image looming at me from the twenty-foot floor-to-ceiling wall mirror. I shuddered and then squared my shoulders.

I told him we were leaving.

"No, we are going to Disney World," he said.

This was the first I had heard anything about Disney World. It felt as though the temperature in the room plummeted as we glared at each other. Our cold words hung in the air. Time and tears froze as we all just stood there.

Finally, Serena, the eldest, soon to turn thirteen and always the peacemaker, stepped up and said, "Daddy, I will stay with you."

He and I shuffled from foot to foot on the polished marble floor. I moved a couple of steps toward the door. He stepped closer. I felt twice threatened—by him and the figure in the mirror.

Nobody was backing down.

He and I just stood there glowering at each other, as the girls looked on, clutching their bags and trying to hold back their tears. The deadlock seemed interminable. I was immobilized and did not know what to do. Back then, I didn't know God well enough to ask for help. It was just me vs. Jacob, my husband of twenty years and, at that moment, a stranger.

I decided to leave Serena with her dad and take Sophia and Leah with me to New Mexico. We loaded the car and started to pull away. Seeing Serena in the driveway waving good-bye made me feel as though I were living a nightmare and being forced to watch my arm being cut off—but not feeling anything because I was numb.

Shaking, I drove to the Tampa airport with my daughters, only to learn that the ordeal wasn't over. The airline official at the desk told me that someone had canceled our tickets. We had no tickets? I held the tickets in my hands, so how could we not have tickets? I challenged the agent. It had to be a mistake.

Jacob had canceled our reservations. It was no mistake. I took a couple of slow breaths to gain control of my emotions—my mind whirled. I couldn't think clearly. Somehow, I managed to purchase new tickets, and we made the trip. My heart was heavy, confused with a swirl of despair, anger, and grief. During the visit, I unloaded every ugly detail of what had happened on my brother and his wife and had many moments when I was sure I could never, never stay married to Jacob.

We returned home, heard from Serena and Jacob that they'd had a nice time at Disney World, and returned to our busy lives. I had learned how to bury painful moments like these beneath the crowded layers of my days.

The Buildup

This specific confrontation was years in the making. Maybe most confrontations are like this. My twin and his wife had two children at the time of the visit, first cousins to my girls but practically strangers. Jacob did not like Danny—or his wife (whom he had never met). That tension had started ten years earlier when we were invited to their wedding. Jacob hadn't wanted to go. The plan was that our daughter Sophia, then nine months old, would stay home with him and our excellent babysitter, while three-year-old Serena and I would fly to California for this weekend trip. Jacob reluctantly went along, at least until he found out that Danny had asked Serena and me to stay in a hotel near his home. His small house couldn't accommodate us. This incensed Jacob. He felt it was unsafe. Furthermore, he considered our staying in a hotel an egregious insult. He was from India, and this arrangement was far from the kind of Indian hospitality that he was accustomed to and that he felt we deserved. I did not appreciate how deeply this hurt him. Serena and I did attend the wedding, and Jacob never forgot it.

As a consequence of that long-ago incident about Danny's wedding, I knew my broaching the subject of a trip to visit New Mexico was fraught with risk. The more I talked about it with Jacob, the more he stonewalled me. Though I feared an explosion, I held my ground. Even now, thirty years later, when I think about this disastrous fight, I feel my jaw tighten and my chest constrict.

Jacob and I couldn't come to an agreement about this family trip, just as we couldn't come to an honest agreement on so many things. We had two decades of experience cementing our poor communication skills. As I try to reconstruct this, I wonder if I went along with him because his ideas or plans were better than mine or just because it was easier to agree. I ask myself, "Did I really want to buy that huge home or the big cars? Did I want to move to Florida? Did I even have an opinion?" I honestly don't know the answers. However, I can appreciate how these habits started during our courtship, when I was more than willing to go along with almost everything this handsome and charming older man wanted.

Life Goes On

I didn't admit it, but in the years following the New Mexico debacle, I increasingly lived two lives. To the world, I was Dr. Chacko, the competent radiation oncologist, wife, and mother of three beautiful daughters—the nice lady who lived in the big, brick waterfront home with the majestic live oak in front. But the high walls around the house hid a different person: a forty-some-year-old who was desperately unhappy, confused, and angry. I did not think Jacob was happy, either. Like me, he was a doctor; his interest was the business end of medicine. He didn't talk much to me about his work, not in the way he talked about investing, in which he clearly found success and which he enjoyed. I knew he loved his children. I thought he loved me as well, but it sometimes seemed he didn't like me too much. I think I loved him, but it was not easy—and I admit there were times when I didn't like him.

We lived in St. Petersburg, Florida, famous for its sunshine and long, white beaches. After several moves, we had finally settled into our beautiful dream home on the edge of Boca Ciega Bay. Our property had dozens of oak and palm trees, a swimming pool with a slide, and a dock. It was postcard perfect and was to be the Chacko finale after many years of education, cross-country moves for medical training, and rental houses. But on the inside things weren't right. It was as though there was a pressure cooker quietly hissing in our home, sometimes harshly, as during the New Mexico fight, inaudible to the outside world.

Jacob and I had been blessed with three daughters, separated by a total of four-and-a-half years. They attracted attention from the time they were little, often being mistaken for triplets. They were striking with their endearing smiles and their olive skin, brown eyes, and long, shiny, dark hair, the product of my husband's East Indian origins and my Anglo-Saxon roots. The girls were friendly and social—later they all ended up on homecoming courts, and two were crowned queens. Starting in middle school, volleyball was their sport—one year their varsity team came in number two at the state championship. Their lives revolved around their friends, volleyball, and their private K–12 college preparatory school, where they excelled.

Their school was a high-pressure place. The students were programmed to compete for top grades, extracurricular honors, success in sports, and social standing. I think this pressure to excel came from all directions: parents, teachers, peers, and the media. Many kids (not ours) received new cars for their sixteenth birthdays. Drinking parties, which started popping up in ninth grade, were highly sought-after weekend destinations. Our girls had no outlets beyond one another and their friends because we had no family in the area, no close family friends, and we participated in no faith community or other groups. The year before the New Mexico trip, I had returned to the Catholic faith of my childhood and registered at a parish. I had never made a conscious decision to abandon God or church, but my life just became too busy and complicated—church fell off the bottom of the to-do list. Over the years, I had taken the children to church only sporadically. They were busy preteens when I finally introduced them to the Catholic Church and its programs. They never felt at home with the church or the youth group.

In spite of all this, the Chacko girls seemed happy. Most of the time I convinced myself that all was well with them. Jacob and I did better as parents when our kids were elementary school age than we did when they were teenagers—it was easier because there were fewer outside pressures and decisions to be made. I look back on those earlier years and see a blur of three precious girls busy with school activities, friends, swimming, gymnastics, talking on the phone, playing with our dogs, or outside activities like fishing with Dad. He taught them to fish with poles and to cast a huge fishing net off our dock to catch mullet. The girls always had projects going, like their classic cooking show in which the guinea pig made a guest appearance on the kitchen counter. Or the time they teamed up with the neighbor girls and made a full production of *Les Misérables*. Do you notice how I tend to lump my daughters together as "the girls," as though they always thought, felt, and desired the same things? This was easy to do because they were close in age and shared interests—and it was convenient. I have a friend who has a private date night with each of her children every year around their birthday. I regret not celebrating the uniqueness of each of my daughters and spending one-on-one time with them when they were young.

Pressure Builds

Soon our daughters were all in middle or high school. They started liking boys, and boys started liking them. This very normal development initiated the most difficult period in our family story. How to parent preteen and teen girls was one of the main things Jacob and I argued about. Though we each deeply loved our girls, we had no ability to discuss, negotiate, weigh pros and cons, and decide on many issues: parties, driving, dating, curfews, joining a club volleyball team, overnight trips, or church participation. Each decision seemed critical—after all, we were talking about our children. Each of us was sure we knew what was best. The problem was that we often didn't agree and had no ability to solve these impasses. He sincerely felt I was too lenient and permissive and that my beliefs would allow ruin to befall our daughters—ruin meaning their having sex or using alcohol or drugs. I believed he was too strict. His desire to be sure they were safe was intense, sometimes leading him to speak loudly and harshly to them as he laid down the rules or quizzed them about their friends. All this is a painful blur. I guess sometimes we agreed and other times one of us would back down, but somehow we always argued.

With hindsight, I now see how striking it is that our children were not and could not be a part of discussions to make decisions so very important to them. Sadly, we rarely included them in our discussions or respectfully listened to their thoughts and needs. That would have been beyond our ability.

The war Jacob and I waged was not a physical battle but a war of words about our daughters and so many other things. It was a war of shouting, silences, and truces. Thank God for the periods of peace in which we enjoyed happy times—like our Saturday early morning outings to the nearby beach two miles from home or longer vacations like cruises or driving trips to Cape Canaveral, St. Augustine, or Busch Gardens.

The litany of topics that Jacob and I could barely talk about extended to my work, such as a particular colleague at my hospital whom he thought was too friendly or decisions about my billing operation about which he wanted more influence. The moment one of these hot-button subjects came near the frontline, my chest tightened. When possible, I adopted the strategy of trying to evade the conversations about these topics. Obviously, this didn't work out too well because life rolled on and decisions and plans had to be made. We even struggled with simple choices, like whether to send the girls to volleyball camp, who would pick them up after their late practice, or where we should go on vacation.

Jacob and I clashed about my family—the hottest of the hot-buttons was my mother. It didn't matter that she and my dad lived 3,000 miles away in Oregon and we rarely saw them. Jacob complained about my mother: "She didn't say hello to me when she called yesterday....Those Christmas ornaments she sends to the kids every year are cheap and insulting....She's always nosey....Why do you want to go and visit?...Why do your parents want to come and visit us?...She's so stingy. Remember that skimpy lunch she made for us before our wedding? What a laugh that was." I can still hear his derisive comments echo in my head. The longer we were married, the more I reacted to these comments. I was long past trying to understand the reason for his complaints or caring about his feelings. I would defend my mom, and soon our conversation would escalate into a loud fight with contorted faces and angry words volleying back and forth. I'd sometimes cry or flee from the room. Over the years our hot words had burned a painful chasm between us that made it impossible to listen or speak to each other about my mother in any way.

Too Busy

Staying busy had been my modus operandi for years. Jacob and I married in 1970, the same year I started medical school. During all our years together, I was either in training or working. I think work helped me avoid thinking about my problems, although I certainly don't recall this being a thought-out strategy. I first became a mother when I was twenty-eight. For each of my three children, I returned to work six weeks after giving birth.

I embraced balancing my responsibilities at home and work and was fortunate because my specialty had few emergencies, and I rarely had to work nights and weekends. We often had daytime help, both for childcare and housework—this freed me from the evening cooking, cleaning, and laundry that weigh down so many working parents. I was very grateful to these women who helped me and lovingly cared for our children.

Growing up in India, Jacob had learned that women take care of the children and the house, even if they work outside the home. It appeared to me this meant that women do everything except manage the money and be in charge. Back when I was in medical school in California in the 1970s, I had witnessed how this played out. We knew a professional couple who were both originally from India. They had two children and equally demanding academic careers at the medical school. I saw that she was in charge of everything at home: cooking, shopping, cleaning, laundry, and everything to do with the children. Decades later this woman and I connected at a professional event. She was divorced. I thought my husband would be different.

On the home front, I had many jobs: food shopping; meal planning or cooking; clothes shopping; helping with school projects; arranging and coordinating transportation for lessons and appointments (doctors, dentists, orthodontists); planning birthday parties; gift buying; planning for Halloween costumes, seasonal celebrations and decorations (especially Christmas); figuring out childcare when they were sick; and making plans for summers and school breaks for the girls. This last duty was particularly wearing. I wanted the girls to be happy, safe, entertained, and maybe even educated during their breaks. I had to consider their desires, availability of camps or in-home childcare, and transportation if they were going to a day program—our babysitter was a big help for the driving. I would end up with something that looked like an Excel sheet to keep track of the arrangements. The girls had many activities, lessons, and games that I attended as often as I could. I think the most fun I had during all these years was attending their volleyball games during middle and high school.

Jacob was not an absentee father—he was home more than I was. He spent time with his girls, for example, on the dock, trying to teach them chess, drawing his funny bird pictures, going to some of their games, or instructing them about money matters. But he was not a partner I could count on to help me with food shopping or any specific task when I was exhausted and needed help. I don't recall his ever helping to get the kids bathed and ready for bed when they were little.

What I remember is always being in a hurry as I juggled my work and family responsibilities. Although I did read to them, I rarely played with my daughters when we were at home together. Instead, I relished having them play together near where I worked in the kitchen or yard: they dressed the dogs; played office with papers and notebooks; made up shows; or created amazing costumes. Once they stuffed the sleeper PJs they were wearing so full of socks and T-shirts that they looked like balloons. I can still hear the loud shouts of "Marco Polo" echoing from the backyard as the girls and their friends played that pool game while I stood at the kitchen window looking out.

I loved my job as a radiation oncologist in my own small department. My office was an oasis, a conflict-free zone with work that was profoundly meaningful to me. I considered it a privilege to be a doctor and valued the relationships with my patients, staff, and colleagues. I had plenty of time to get to know each patient, and it was very satisfying to be able to help them. It was a huge responsibility to be in charge of someone's cancer treatment and to remain up to date with the medical literature. But this was easy compared to the pressures I felt in my marriage and home life.

Breaking Point

I was weary. Emotionally and physically. But it wasn't the fatigue that would break me. It was that I could no longer bear the anxiety I felt about my children. More and more I agonized about how the longstanding war between my husband and me was affecting them. More and more I thought he was too hard on them—but we remained unable to effectively communicate about our differences. In his fierce desire to keep his girls safe, his words became more cutting, both to them and to their friends. His concerns sometimes led to suspicious questioning of his daughters after they returned home from an activity or to eavesdropping on their conversations. I can still hear the echoes of his booming questions and accusations: "Who was at the party? Where else did you go? Was Bob there? Who was drinking? Why can't he identify himself on the phone? That music is crude."

I cannot recall what I was saying or doing during these episodes—if I was yelling or cowering. I also don't really know what Jacob thought about my mothering, although I do recall him telling me I put pleasing other people ahead of our daughters' best interests. I thought I was a good mother and focused only on Jacob's fathering. As far as our daughters could see, we were a team, albeit a messed-up one. I blamed Jacob for all the dysfunction of our team—in the same way that he no doubt blamed me.

It was years later when I came to realize how unavailable I was to my daughters; I was either working, busy at home, or just unable to listen—maybe because I was afraid of what I would hear.

So, as a family, we lumbered onward, a slow-motion march to predictable disaster. I was increasingly miserable and also began to wonder if Jacob was more than unhappy, possibly depressed. I felt helpless. I prayed more but didn't hear answers. I cried, often while sitting on my bedroom floor in the middle of the night reading the poems and inspirational prayers I had collected and hid in my closet in a cardboard box. One prayer I treasured had been my grandma's and hung in her bedroom, the words imprinted on leather: "Lord, for tomorrow and its needs I do not pray…keep me, my God…just for today." I think this is also when I first stumbled onto the Serenity Prayer by Reinhold Niebuhr:

> God, grant me the serenity to accept
> the things I cannot change,
> the courage to change the things I can,
> and the wisdom to know the difference.

During those times I heard no answers from God and felt only brief solace from my prayers. I sought professional counseling and read many self-help books. I reached out to smiley Kathy, a petite, older woman whom I met in a Bible study group at church. We spent special time drinking tea and chatting at her kitchen table, and I found much comfort in her listening ear and her faith. But I still didn't know what to do.

I felt as though I needed to flail at somebody or something. Sometimes I wanted to hit Jacob. I would feel my body tighten as I muzzled my anger. A couple of times his hard face and tense body made me think he had similar thoughts—he looked like a loaded slingshot ready to fire. I vividly remember one evening when we stood in our bedroom arguing about the children—we tautly held our arms up with elbows bent in a defensive posture, like boxers. We tried to grab each other's forearms, partially succeeding. That was the only time we physically touched each other in anger. It was frightening. My long-suppressed resentment and anger at Jacob, and maybe myself, was building up. Now the pressure cooker was hissing a shrill warning—the heat was turned up too high.

I raged at Jacob, my husband of more than twenty years, and I raged at God. My anguish about my children was unbearable. I felt as though I were on the edge of a dark pit, looking down and worrying that the girls would fall into the muck.

Looking Back

During those awful times, I was not thinking clearly. My mind was a tangle of feelings and thoughts that made no sense. God seemed far away. I didn't understand how I came to be clinging to the edge of that dark pit. I didn't even want to understand. I only wanted solutions.

It took years before I realized I would have to go back to the very beginning to find answers.

2

————•—•——

Becoming Me

"One, so far."

That was the nurse's hurried announcement of my arrival into this world, addressed to my waiting father. No one had been expecting twins! The scene was Portland, Oregon, 1949. The end of World War II had allowed my parents, and many others, to finally start their families. My twin, Danny, and I joined the baby boomers, along with our seventeen-month-old brother, Dave. Mom was thirty-eight years old.

I've always thought of my childhood as happy. When I shut my eyes and look back, I see myself playing outside with my brothers. We trampled trails in the fields of tall grass so we could play in the maze, climbed our fruit trees, and then gorged on the apples and plums, and constructed bridges and dams in the ever-present Portland mud puddles. I played dolls incessantly with my friend who lived across the street, while my brothers were more drawn to digging holes, climbing things, and, later, exploding things. My parents loved boats and the Columbia River, located not far from where we lived in Northeast Portland. As kids,

we fished, water-skied, raced up and down the sand
and sometimes buried ourselves in squishy, wet sand we
pretended was quicksand.

My brothers and I were granted considerable freedom.
As we got older we could ride our bikes as far as we wanted,
as long as we returned by dinner. Our mom did not hover
or rescue—once I was stranded for what seemed hours on
the roof of the "pig house," a decrepit outbuilding behind
our home. Mom's view was that, since I got up, I should
be able to get down. When I was about six, I was climbing on the chain-link fence behind our property, where
I wasn't supposed to be. I wanted to pet the horses that
had been temporarily placed there. One horse, apparently
drawn by my cranberry-red dress, pranced over to me and
grabbed the gathered skirt into his mouth. In an instant
the entire front of my skirt was gone. I screamed in fear
and shock, wailing as I ran toward the house. Mom, who
was in the house calmly sewing, heard me coming and
just waited, mysteriously having determined that no grave
injury had occurred. When I finally got into the house
and approached her, I sobbed, "The horse ate my dress!"
Her response was her classic line, spoken without rising
from her chair: "Oh, come over to me so I can pick you
up." She enjoyed retelling that story, and each time it made
me a little uncomfortable. I could have been embarrassed
or maybe part of me wondered why she hadn't gotten up
and rushed to offer me comfort?

Our grandparents lived five blocks away. When I got to
be eight, I could walk alone to their house. Staying all night
with Grandma and Grandpa was a special treat. Grandma
made yeasty homemade bread; Grandpa had a woodworking
shop complete with the rich smell of its wood-burning stove;

and, they always had a braided-silver dish full of mints on the corner table of the living room. I loved my grandparents but cannot recall sharing my problems with them.

In the early years, the large, yellow bookmobile came regularly to our block. Later we made frequent jaunts to our airy and modern public library. We all loved to read, which was a good thing since it rained all the time in Portland and there often was nothing else to do. My favorite reading spot was the upholstered armchair by the corner window in the living room. I spent hours reading in this cushy chair, my legs draped sidewise over its arms. My early favorites were Beverly Cleary's books about Ramona Quimby, *The Secret Garden,* and *Heidi.*

This was the pretechnology era. The first phone I remember was a "party line" we shared with a family of strangers; later we had our private landline. TV appeared in our home when I was six years old, a twelve-inch, black-and-white screen that auspiciously brought the well-known Catholic Bishop Fulton Sheen into our home the very first time we flipped the "on" switch. Every Friday night Grandma and Grandpa's 1938 Oldsmobile rumbled into the drive so Grandpa and Dad could watch Friday night boxing on the TV. The radio and record player cabinet in the living room had push-buttons that made a satisfying snap when pressed—but I don't recall the radio ever working.

My brothers and I enjoyed remarkable family stability. We lived in the same home throughout our growing up years. Our parents stayed married and lived in that same home for all their years together. Dad remained at the same job at a printing factory. Mom stayed home, except for her work helping with Dad's home printing business, his second job, and her volunteer activities for our school and church.

While we were never rich, we never felt poor or financially insecure. We all attended the same Catholic grade school until I went to the girls' Catholic high school and my brothers went to the boys' Catholic high school. There was no major illness in our family except for our elderly grandparents getting sick and dying while we were in our teens. Mom and Dad spent many happy hours with us for family outings on the boat, but also picnics, camping trips, and salmon fishing trips at the coast, always accompanied by our loyal black lab, Duffy.

Work

My parents and grandparents spoke the same language about work: anything you do is worth doing well; maintain your property; repair things that break; clean up your messes; take care of your tools. The post-Depression work ethic ran strong in both generations. They passed it on to my brothers and me. The boys helped Dad, I helped Mom, but we all had a share of housework and yardwork. My mom, an expert seamstress, taught me to sew. Starting in grade school, I made much of my own clothing. As my brothers and I got older, we helped more with the home printing business. We folded printed papers or we collated stacks of printed papers, taking the white and pink sheets and restacking them so the colors would alternate in the stack. The fun part was rubbing sticky glycerin on our fingers so we could more easily pick up each paper.

I regularly babysat, but I never made much money. In fact, I still remember my angst when, at age fifteen, I finally worked up enough courage to ask the neighbor for a raise to 45 cents an hour for my summer babysitting job. My mom had told me it never hurts to ask, as long as you ask nicely. My brothers had paper routes for years; then they both worked at a local steak restaurant. After taking piano lessons a few years, I started getting paid to play the organ at church at the earliest Sunday Mass. I cringe when I think how little I knew about music and organs in particular. One time I even played at a wedding and obliviously selected the graduation march *Pomp and Circumstance* as the processional song. But our most impressive childhood work experience was strawberry picking. In the summers, starting in grade school, my brothers and I rode off early with the other neighborhood kids in a big bus. Wearing our oldest tattered clothes and floppy hats, we willingly went off for our stint of child labor. An extraordinarily remunerative day would bring in $4.50, but usually we earned $1.50-$3.00. This was hard and dirty work, crawling on our knees between the long rows of berry plants in the full sun, dragging our wooden crates along. Our crumpled-up, juice-stained dollars looked like blood money. I recently discovered some berry juice stains left in my diary from when I entered my earnings. We continued this work for several summers and just took it in stride.

My summer job right after high school was as a "Kelly Girl," working in a huge typing pool with dozens of other young women, typing (on manual typewriters) multicopy insurance policies using carbon paper. We typed detailed descriptions of jewelry, silver, and other valuables on these homeowners' policies. Any typing error was disastrous because of the multiple copies. But what I most recall about that job is how intimidated I was by those older girls, so experienced in the world with their boyfriends, nail polish, and 1960s bouffant hair. Their clothes seemed so sophisticated—short skirts and sweaters that showed off the figure, something I didn't yet claim. At lunch, I sat alone in the breakroom with my instant tomato soup, hard-boiled egg, and book.

Our parents' philosophy about schoolwork was similar to their approach to work in general. Mom and Dad were both very smart, but because of the Depression and the war, neither had advanced beyond high school. Their messaging about the need for us to excel at school was an unambiguous, ever-present expectation of achievement rather than spoken exhortations, threats, or rewards. Even now, I don't really understand how they communicated this expectation to us. But my brothers and I certainly got the message.

High School

In 1963, during my freshman year of high school, President John F. Kennedy was assassinated. The first year after high school, Rev. Martin Luther King and Senator Robert Kennedy were assassinated. I sometimes marvel at my happy memories of those high school years—bookmarked as they were by assassinations and crammed with social and political turmoil. There were riots. The Vietnam War raged—in my junior year my older brother was deployed to Vietnam as a Marine. He came back whole. His high school friend came back with no legs. His Marine buddy did not come back at all. The civil rights movement in the United States peaked at this same time. George Wallace blocked integration at the University of Alabama in 1963. The March on Washington and MLK's "I Have a Dream" speech occurred that same year. Malcolm X was killed in 1965. I knew not one person of color until I started high school, when I had one African American classmate whom I barely knew. I am embarrassed to admit how removed I was from the civil rights movement. At the time, I was having fun in high school with plenty of girlfriends and activities. My parents didn't appear to be interested in politics or world affairs. We didn't talk about these things, although I was aware that Mom was a Democrat and Dad was a Republican. It was an anomaly when Dad called us into the dining room in 1962 to inform us of the Cuban Missile Crisis and the grave risk of war. The somber faces on my brothers, then twelve and fourteen years old, didn't match their playful freckles and Dennis the Menace hair.

There was one problem, however. I was becoming convinced that I was not appealing to boys. I wasn't pretty enough. I started my teens wearing ugly, blue-and-white-striped glasses and braces. I was mortified by my tiny breasts, and I continually compared my flat chest to the curves of my classmates. I intently studied the glossy photos of *Teen* magazine to which I subscribed. The girls all looked perfect. I was also the last to get my period—not until I was nearly seventeen. Lacking this badge of womanhood, I felt less feminine than the other girls—I was different. Inferior. I was embarrassed and ashamed. Not being asked to dance at the post-game sock hops was a painful reinforcement of that negative self-image. I remember sulking in the hot and crowded gym. Part of me tried to merge with the other wallflowers so as to be invisible, but another part tried to smile and look whatever popular looked like. If anyone later asked about the dance, I would just say, "Oh, it was OK," but inside, the humiliation was crushing. It didn't help that I was smart, since I believed boys didn't like brainy girls.

But the fact is, I did have boyfriends in high school, including Jim for almost two years. He was a great guy and attended my brothers' high school, where he played football. But over time I found myself being annoyed by the way he laughed and his unruly hair. Like a few others, Jim's name was grayed out in my ledger of boyfriends. He filled a space, but not a need. For reasons I don't understand, he didn't count.

During high school, I was a high performer. I had the advantages of a solid family, good genes, and a great education—I graduated as the valedictorian of the class of 1967. But the truth was that I was an insecure and naive eighteen-year-old as I geared up to attend Oregon State University in the fall.

Spiritual Roots

It was in Catholic grade school for eight years and then in an all-girls Catholic high school for four years that I learned about my faith. In grade school we had daily Mass at 8:15 a.m. before school started. Those were the days of the mandatory lace head covering for girls and the fat daily missals with the cool, colored ribbons to mark the pages. Those also were the years of my First Communion, and later, the sacrament of Confirmation—the details of which are vague in my memory. I know the last name of my godparents. But honestly, I don't ever remember meeting them. However, I do remember that I got to wear nylon stockings and a garter belt for the first time at my Confirmation. In school we learned about God, prayer, Bible stories, and the teachings of the church. One time our class went on a retreat, maybe in eighth grade. During the program, I felt a strong calling to make a commitment to God, but experienced a powerful resistance. As I try to reconstruct what happened, I think it was something like an altar call that I just couldn't make myself answer, as much as I wanted to. I dug in my heels, pressed into my chair, and struggled to make a decision. I remember the discomfort of that tug of war with God, but cannot recall if I ever did stand up and join the others in front. This wouldn't be the last time I felt that kind of strong internal resistance to saying "yes" to God.

My brothers and I always went to Sunday Mass with Mom; Dad was not a Catholic. We did not pray as a family, nor did we talk about God, as far as I can recall. The exception was that I would occasionally pray the rosary with Grandma when I stayed at her house—kneeling by her bed. I can still see the soft, brown beads in her wrinkled fingers and smell her ever-present lavender soap. Today on my bedroom wall hangs the small sepia image of Mary and the baby Jesus that Grandma had in her bedroom. It makes me smile when I look at it.

I mentioned we always went to Mass on Sundays with Mom. The odd thing was that she never received Holy Communion. One day I finally got brave enough to ask her why. She awkwardly told me of her doubts about the sacrament, shocking me into silence by saying she wondered if eating the Communion wafer wasn't something like cannibalism. Years later, when I was sixteen or seventeen, I was reminded of that strange conversation. In an unrelated discussion, my mom casually mentioned something about her first husband. Her first husband? Mom had been divorced? I gasped. My mind whirled. This couldn't be. Not my mother! I could only think of one person I knew who had been divorced. For months after this revelation, when I looked at Mom, I saw a stranger. She was still a tall, erect, capable woman. But now I saw a divorcee instead of my mother. I was disoriented and confused. Somehow, in this fog, I realized that this first marriage had prevented her from marrying my father in the Catholic Church—and, as a consequence, from receiving Communion. This was so sad, yet we never talked about it—like so many other things. The story reveals much about the awkward relationship our family had with faith and religion.

I approached religion and God as I approached school. I needed to follow the rules and get points by doing the right thing so I could reach the goal—in this case, heaven. I did pray, but I don't recall feeling close to Jesus or trusting him. I do remember frequently being worried about my behaviors and often feeling guilty. People joke about Catholics and our guilt. But it's not funny. I confess that one time I took a small holy card off the mantel at my neighbor's house and felt guilty for years. Hyperacute, old-school Catholic guilt is baggage I still carry around, although with maturity and prayer I have significantly downsized my bag. It would take many years before I understood the unconditional love of Jesus.

When I look back at the early years of my spiritual life, I feel gratitude. My parents taught me how to live a moral life, both by word and example. My Catholic education and the kind Dominican nuns helped me put down my baby spiritual roots. My early religious education taught me some key points: God loves us, and he asks us to love him, to love others, to forgive, and not to lie or steal. My faith seedlings were planted in abundant soil, so they did survive, but somehow I wasn't ready to till the ground, water, fertilize, weed, and do all that would have helped my faith grow. As you will see, life just became too busy.

Missing Pieces

Despite all the good, there were some missing pieces—and this is hard for me to admit. My parents loved me and provided for me, but I gradually realized there were identifiable missing or imperfect pieces in the story. This isn't all bad—I am who I am because of all the pieces, perfect, flawed, and missing.

We were not a physically affectionate family. We did give and receive the routine hug or kiss, but these signs of affection were not the warm, cozy type that make you want to linger or do it again. We didn't cuddle on the couch. Mom and Dad didn't often display physical affection, other than a quick peck and hug. As youngsters, we never joined them in their bed in the mornings. Affectionate touch was infrequent. During those years I didn't recognize this lack of physical affection as a problem. It was just the way it was.

Our parents did not feel comfortable talking with us about feelings or difficult subjects, especially sex. One time, after building up my courage for weeks, I clumsily asked my mom what a homosexual was (I got that word from my favorite newspaper advice column). She deflected the question and didn't answer. I still remember standing by the dining room table where she was sitting. I looked down, feeling overwhelmed with some uncomfortable emotion that might have been embarrassment or shame—then I retreated. She never taught me about the birds and the bees, and I never asked. Years later I asked my brothers about their sex education. They said Dad had sent them to our family doctor for this purpose. The doc asked them if they had questions, they said no, and that was the beginning and end of their formal sex education. We didn't have sex education in school, either. Even getting close to that subject was taboo. Once someone asked one of the nuns in religion class what "circumcision" was. This prompted an embarrassed, mumbled non-answer from that befuddled, red-faced, elderly sister who kept her eyes glued to the floor during the entire exchange. When I was in eighth grade, while walking home from school, a man exposed himself to me. I never told anyone. During my school years I learned about the biology of reproduction. But it was at a high-school slumber party when I really got it. I recall screeching, "Really?!?!? That's how it works?"

Recently our neighbor's aging dog had to be put to sleep, and she was very concerned that her son should return home beforehand so they could talk about it and share the painful experience. I immediately remembered our loyal black Duffy dog and his last days. One summer day, one of my brothers said, "Hey, Mom, where's Duffy? I can't find him." She turned and said, "Well, you must not be too worried, because you didn't notice he's been gone a few days. He was getting too old and sick, so I took him to the vet to be put to sleep." I recall immediately feeling guilty, certain I was a bad girl who didn't care or even notice that our dear Duffy was gone. I don't recall saying anything, just silently shrinking away to feel sad and confused by myself.

As far as corporal punishment goes, I only recall a passing swipe on the butt from Mom or Dad when I was young. My brothers did receive physical punishment from our father with the leather shaving strap, but it was rare, and I was hardly aware at the time—nobody talked about it.

Our family of five had close and frequent ties only to Grandma and Grandpa and an adopted aunt—that's what my brothers and I knew as our family. Mom had no living siblings, her great sorrow being the 1930 drowning of her only brother, Fred, at age twenty. Up until her death at age ninety, Mom would get teary-eyed talking about Fred and how her father had dragged the Columbia River with his boat for weeks looking for Fred's never-found body. Dad lost both his parents and his favorite sister while he was in northern India during World War II. His older sister and brother-in-law, along with their two children, actually lived in Portland, but I only recall seeing them a couple of times while growing up. They were strangers to me. We maintained contact with our great aunt and uncle in Victoria, British Columbia, but other aunts, uncles, nieces, and nephews were dead or lived far away. I assumed we didn't travel or visit on long-distance phone calls because of expense. I don't remember my parents ever talking about the importance of staying connected or the value of prioritizing family above all else.

When I hear an adult speak lovingly of their parent, particularly their mom, as their "best friend" and of missing them intensely every single day after their death, I feel wistful because my mother wasn't my best friend, and I don't have those feelings. I certainly loved and respected my long-departed mother, but she was no soul mate or confidante. Is this because of how she raised me? Or, was it me? Was I just a cold person who couldn't love properly? Maybe I didn't learn as a child how to have deep, intimate relationships. After I left home, geographical distance, busyness, and family conflict hampered my ability to build a closer relationship with my parents. We always stayed in regular touch, but I feel much sadness about the distance between us.

Mom lovingly cared for Dad during many years of illness that started right after his retirement. I think they were faithful to each other to the end. But it appeared that she often went along with Dad in order to get along. Tensions were sometimes evident. We might have witnessed Dad being curt, Mom looking tense or suffering migraines, or a frigid silence between them, but we never saw fights. Only once do I remember Mom getting really angry. At what, I don't know. We were in the backyard cleaning up after a picnic. She was carrying a stack of plates back toward the house. Something set her off, and she hurled the whole stack of plates to shatter on the ground. Years later, sticking to my "delay and then ask" routine, I inquired about this incident. She just said they were old dishes and ready to be discarded.

My sister-in-law used to aggravate me by declaring Mom was passive-aggressive. Maybe she was right. Clearly my parents didn't model for us what a healthy communication style looks like in a strong marriage. They no doubt learned their style from their own parents, all of whom had been born in the 1800s.

Unconditional love was not explicitly expressed. There was a certain distance to be maintained between our parents and my brothers and me. They were not harsh or critical, at least with me. But our parents' expectations were made clear: we were to do our work and do it well, earn money, be frugal, and be respectful. Was their love conditional on my brothers and me fulfilling these expectations? They never said so, but I wonder. Their expectations came through loud and clear, and I don't recall hearing the words "I love you" in our home. Nor do I remember the feeling of being comforted. On the other hand, their actions seemed to show they deeply loved us no matter what. We constantly observed them showing their love by spending time with us, teaching us, providing us a dog and a stable home, and sacrificing to send us to Catholic schools.

The arts were not part of our family culture. No music from records or radio filled the communal space, although you might have heard me practicing the piano. I am grateful that I was able to take piano lessons from one of the nuns for five years. I wasn't exposed to classical music and still don't have much interest in it. Although our parents did not emphasize art, writing, or creativity for its own sake, they were highly creative and ingenious when it came to solving problems, fixing things, sewing, and accomplishing all types of home projects.

Finally, I don't recall a lot of humor in our home. It's not that we didn't laugh and have fun, but playfulness, bantering, gags, and clowning around were just not our style.

Looking Back

This is how I came to be who I am, like a beautiful puzzle formed with mostly good pieces, some defective pieces, and several missing pieces, but all glued together with good intentions and love. When I reflect on my growing-up years, I feel profound gratitude and compassion for my parents. They weathered the Depression, suffered through World War II, and endured painful losses of family members. They worked very, very hard their entire lives and provided a stable, loving home and excellent education for me and my brothers. My family of origin provided many advantages to me those first eighteen years. My brothers and I spread out after high school and saw little of one another for a number of years. Fortunately, there was no rift, only distance.

Unlike so many others, I never had to deal with divorce, violence, addiction, or abuse. In spite of these advantages,

I did leave home with a few not-so-healthy ingrained patterns of thinking. I believed boys wouldn't like me because I was somehow deficient and unappealing. I was oblivious to another tendency, which would later cause me much grief: my need to avoid confrontation—I thought I was just being nice and polite.[1] I thought my drive to always work hard was a great asset. I didn't realize the unconscious and unhealthy motivations that often drove my need to be productive. Critically, I did not carry from home a belief that I was unconditionally loved or lovable, independent of my performance.

My parents, like me and all parents, weren't perfect. This imperfect parenting contributed to unconscious imprints in me that I carried into adulthood—when they presented as unhealthy patterns of thinking. I agree with the notion that imperfect parenting, with its effects on children, is perpetrated over and over in successive generations, by all parents, as part of our human condition.

All this contributed to personal problems in my life. The good news is that these same problems eventually drove me to seek a better path.

---

1. Evelyn Sommers, *Tyranny of Niceness* (Dundurn Press, 2005), description of the social dysfunction that is created by too much niceness.

3

Six-and-a-Half Weeks

I vividly recall the drive on I-5 from Portland to Corvallis, Oregon, home of Oregon State University, riding between Mom and Dad in the front seat of our boat-size, forest-green Mercury. The back seat was jammed with a clothing rack and all my things. I remember pulling up to the crowded drive in front of West Hall, which would be my home for the next two years. After that first day, my memories of OSU are sketchy. My gestalt has always been that I studied all the time, didn't have much of a social life, and got fat because I ate too much. But my diaries told a different story about some of these things.

I did study way more than most other students. I had decided on a premed major because, as I accurately said, "I like science and I like people." I worked hard, usually in the library or in the tiny study cubicles in the dorm basement, isolated and strategically near the vending machines. I remember eating five or six doughnuts or goodies from the machines, like Hostess cupcakes, apple pies, or Butterfinger bars. I followed that with a starvation diet to "make up." This meant that I fasted or ate a salad or a hotdog. I remember digging into the huge tub of peanut butter and mountains of Wonder bread that were the centerpiece of the large dining hall during lunch.

What I did not recall and was saddened to read much later in my diary was the extent of my self-loathing about my overeating. I recorded in detail the many days "I ate," "What a fool!" "Such a dope!" Yes, I did gain weight, but the 130-140 pound weights I carefully recorded in my diary were far lower than my recollection. This cycling between overeating and dieting was very prominent during my first and second years in college. It became less marked with time, but endured until my children were born years later. After that time I gradually reverted to fairly normal eating habits.

I photoshopped this memory for years, seeing myself only as someone with temporarily unhealthy eating habits. Even when my oldest daughter was diagnosed with an eating disorder, I still didn't fully admit to myself that I too had suffered from one. I recognize that I have always valued slimness. My family was slim. Slimness was healthy. Obesity was unhealthy. I thought my preference for slimness was all about health. Gradually I realized how conditioned I was to equate thinness with beauty and discipline. Now I have a much better understanding of the complex roots of obesity.

The biggest discrepancy between my memory and the facts recorded in my diary is how much social life I had. I "clearly" remember that I rarely went out on a date, had no close friends, and that I was on the sophomore homecoming "Betty Coed" court as a fluke that had nothing to do with positive attributes or popularity. These perceptions were entered into my memory bank in indelible black ink. But the Donna who lived in my diaries had lots of dates and boyfriends while at OSU. She went to fraternity parties, movies, and concerts. She participated in student activities and enjoyed time with girlfriends.

Interestingly, there was one college escapade that I do remember in living color. It was hopping the freight train. Four couples, including me and my then boyfriend, Keith, came up with this idea. We decided to hop on the train as it came through our college "cow-town" of Corvallis, going west toward the coast. We walked downtown, staked out our spot, and waited. We heard the rumbling of the distant train. As it grew louder and closer, we spied a freight car with its sliding doors ajar. We skittered across the road to catch it. I was shocked how high freight trains are, much higher than they look. Getting aboard the train, even though it was moving slowly, was no easy task. Some of us, me included, needed to be hauled up by others onto the rough wooden floor of the empty, dank car. The ride through the Oregon Coast range was beautiful. I remember seeing the snow blankets on the evergreen boughs as we sped by. They were so close we could practically touch them—the door was partly open. We chug-a-lugged through the forest, extinguishing the silence with our metallic clanging. The air inside the freight car was frozen, and we huddled together to stay warm. When the train stopped at Toledo, Oregon, a town that was even smaller than Corvallis, we jumped off. Fortunately, the town had a laundromat, and it was open. What I remember next is the warm, cozy feeling of being in the clothes dryer in that laundromat. Could we really have climbed into the clothes dryer for warmth? Preposterous as it sounds, that is what I remember—though I must admit the dryer wasn't mentioned in my detailed diary account. I can't overstate how proud of myself I was after this caper—and still am. Could it be because this was the one time I broke free from the unconscious requirement that I be smart and good?

I didn't drink too much. I wrote in my diaries about folks getting drunk at parties, and one time I described a drinking fraternity party where I held my one beer all night long. I only recall getting really drunk one time, an experience I sickeningly recall and which my diary details in all its ugliness. At a party I drank white wine on an empty stomach, got very, very sick, and then rode laid out in the back seat of someone's car on a visit home to Portland. I still don't like white wine. Somehow I bypassed the whole drug scene.

While I did love kissing and often noted in my diary about which guys were the best kissers, I was clear that I wasn't going to have sex with any of these guys. Without any sex education or meaningful conversation about the gift of sexuality, I had a limited understanding of sex and what a healthy, loving sex life really meant.

In the late '60s, politics was difficult to avoid. The civil rights movement was in full swing. Martin Luther King Jr. was killed and riots broke out in our cities. Protests against the Vietnam War were raging. It was during college that I started to get involved in politics for the first time. When Eugene McCarthy decided in 1967 to enter the primary race for president as an anti-war candidate against President Johnson, I, and many young people, rallied for him and with him. In spring 1968, I traveled to campaign for him—causing me to miss several exams. Senator Robert Kennedy entered the primary in March 1968. When he was assassinated in June 1968, I felt empty and raw, as if some important part of my inner self had been forcibly sucked out of me. I felt a special bond with Senator Kennedy because I had touched his white, starched shirt cuff at a crowded rally in Portland. It seemed so soon after President Kennedy's assassination. I wondered what was happening to the world. It's hard to know how these events affected me, but I'm sure they had something to do with my lifelong interest in current affairs and politics.

The premed curriculum was demanding. When I look back I see such a paradox between the naive and insecure teenager that I was and the smart, responsible, disciplined student that I also was. Unfortunately, my doubts about my academic abilities grew during these years, an experience I later realized was shared by many other young women.[2] It drove me to study even more, often in eight- to ten-hour chunks. I had moved from an all-girl high school to a male-dominated world: most of my premed classmates were male; the faculty was all male; the program was designed by men; I had not one female mentor and, in fact, had never even met a female physician. As far as the burgeoning women's movement, I thought I was doing my part for women by pursuing a profession; I didn't really identify with the feminist movement.

I celebrated my twentieth birthday, completed my second year of college, and looked forward to summer at home. I would have been flabbergasted if you told me that six-and-a-half weeks later I would be engaged.

---

2. Gloria Steinem, *Revolution from Within, A Book of Self-Esteem,* (Open Road Media, 2012), 124-125.

The Decision

I returned home to Portland for summer break and my waiting job. On June 14, 1969, I helped a boyfriend move out of his apartment. That night I went to what I described in my diary as "a groovey party" at the home of a high-school girlfriend, whose older sister's friends were in attendance. These guys were graduate students at the University of Oregon School of Medicine, located in Portland. I was in awe. The medical school—this was the major league. One of them was Jacob, a doctorate student, who soon started calling me. In an uncanny coincidence, my summer job was located at the medical school near Jacob's office. I had never met anyone even remotely similar to Jacob. Ten years earlier he had immigrated to the United States from Kerala, India, and then worked to support himself, travel the world, and complete his education. The youngest of a large family in India, his parents already had died, his mother only the preceding year. He was a charming, thirty-year-old, dark-skinned man with a beard and a wide smile that revealed big, white teeth. He was ready to settle down, and he wanted me. I was very flattered. I couldn't believe it. A world-traveled sophisticate who was ten years my senior and about to complete his PhD at the medical school really liked me. I enjoyed my time with him, and with time I came to love him. I think.

I met a few of his friends, but none of his family. He clearly was a hard worker. He didn't appear to be a spendthrift. He was not a churchgoer, but he was raised as a Christian and described his mother as kind and saintly. I saw no red flags as the relationship started to bloom. We saw each other regularly at work and went out often in the evening, to movies or dinner, usually alone. I visited his apartment—that is where we watched the July 1969 moon landing.

One of our first dates was to see the movie *Goodbye, Columbus*. I wrote in my diary: "The relationship amazes me—like a little girl dating a professor…it sure would be easy to fall in love with Jacob." I described him as "loving and considerate."

Everything wasn't perfect, however. During those early days I wrote in my diary about upsetting him because I needed some space and only wanted to go out with him on Friday or Saturday nights, not both. I did not stick with this preference for longer than one weekend. Later, after we had gone to a party together, I wrote: "Jacob was possessive and it bothered me."

The courtship was short, six-and-a-half weeks, but it was long enough for me to go on three dates with two guys other than Jacob. The last was a picnic with Jim, about which I wrote: "a picnic of cheese, bread, fruit and wine. Ah, romantic. I sure like [Jim], a nice guy, that's for sure." Three days after that, I wrote about Jacob, "When I am with Jacob I think I love him," and later, "I think I am falling in love with Jacob and it is beautiful!"

It was nine days after that memorable picnic with Jim that I looked at engagement rings with Jacob. The very next day Jacob proposed to me, and I said "yes." Even now when I read this, I just shake my head in amazement.

I don't know where I stashed my early doubts and questions—clearly in some well-fortified hiding place. I don't think I had enough self-confidence to admit my doubts or need for more time. A few weeks into the relationship with Jacob I admitted my unhealthy state of mind in my diary: "I cannot stand myself any longer and am a fat slob who is, thus far, wasting her summer away." Certainly not the sentiment of a self-assured, well-adjusted young woman.

The engagement was official. My parents briefly protested, but capitulated. We set a date for the following spring. This all happened so fast. I guess my need for acceptance, security, and manly love was more urgent than my need to be cautious in making what may be the most important single decision a young person can make. Searching my diary I didn't find passionate declarations of undying love for Jacob. But I wrote that I loved him, and I really think that I did. He had many attractive qualities. I guess I was afraid to question anything, knowing I would then have to face the conflict or risk losing him. I was establishing a pattern that would be very difficult to change.

Yoked

In September, proudly flashing my engagement ring, I returned to Corvallis to start my junior year. Jacob stayed in Portland working hard to complete his doctoral thesis. I was very busy because I was trying to complete the premed requirements in three years, rather than the usual four, having learned that I might be accepted to medical school without actually graduating. I've tried to reconstruct my motivation for rushing through my education: to save time; to save money; and, I also remember thinking I needed to shorten my education in order to beat my biological clock—just in case. The last is odd, because I also remember thinking that my decision to become a doctor would mean I couldn't/wouldn't be married.

Because I was living two hours away from Portland, Jacob thought I needed a car. He bought me a 1960 light green Corvair. His expectation was that my parents would pay for the car insurance since he had bought the car. They declined, he railed, and I was confused, vacillating in my head between "He shouldn't have assumed they would pay without discussing it first," and "Mom and Dad really should pay." Jacob remained angry about this episode for decades. I regularly shuttled back and forth between Corvallis and Portland in my little Corvair, and Jacob visited me as well. I continued to sporadically write in my diary and on Oct. 7 described one of his visits: "We went to the symphony...he came here—and I slept with him. First time. Very cozy. I sure wish, sometimes, that I wasn't a virgin." We really did just sleep. I wrote often about Jacob, how much I loved him, the three knit tops he bought me, the time he drove to Corvallis because I was having a terrible day. On December 28, 1969, the last day I ever wrote in my diary, I said, "Spent a lot of time at Jacob's—our relationship is a beautiful thing!" The diary no longer described the occasional doubt or concern that had been noted during the summer courtship.

We set our wedding date for the following March. It would be a Catholic wedding at a small chapel on the grounds of a small college in North Portland, where Jacob was teaching part-time. I had wanted to be married in my home parish where I had grown up, gone to school, played the organ, and where my mom still attended. However, our introductory visit with the longtime pastor did not go well. The priest immediately voiced his disapproval of all birth control. The pill had first been available in 1960 and by this time was widely in use. Jacob became perturbed. I was dismayed—about the priest's seeming intransigence, even after I told him I would be starting medical school; about Jacob's huffy reaction; and about the lost prospect of being married in the only church I had ever known. We quickly left the rectory and made alternative plans.

The Transfer

Jacob soon began encouraging me to transfer from OSU to Portland State University (PSU) in January for what we hoped would be my last required semester before medical school, assuming I got accepted. He said it would be more convenient if I were in Portland for the months leading up to our March wedding. I remember initially resisting the transfer to Portland for that one semester, which was to have been my last semester at OSU. I ultimately agreed that the move from Corvallis back to Portland was the most "practical" thing. That word "practical" will come up again.

After making the move, I enrolled at PSU in January 1970. This was a stressful change for many reasons. I had to drive to downtown Portland each day for classes. Everything was unfamiliar, and I knew no one. The required classes at OSU and PSU didn't correspond with each other. The biggest mismatch was Organic Chemistry. I had taken Organic Chemistry 1 at OSU without a lab component, and then transferred into the same class at PSU—except the students at PSU already had taken a full semester of lab. Chemistry was not an easy subject for me. Being thrown into that lab made me feel like Daniel in the lions' den. There were mainly guys in the class, guys who seemed very smart and not very helpful. I fumbled with the equipment. Did the pipette go into the Erlenmeyer flask? What was a burette? I keenly remember how I felt in the lab: clumsy, self-conscious, stupid, and fat. Somehow they all went together, one and the same. One particular memory stands out. I was standing at the lab bench trying to figure out what to do, while at the same time thinking about how fat and ugly I looked in the dress I was wearing that day. I had made the dress. It was a muddy brown color, and it looked like a loose flannel sack except for the adjustable chain link belt around the middle.

My memories of wedding preparations are hazy. Maybe we had a shower or a rehearsal dinner. I just can't remember. Maybe I was too busy to be excited. But I do remember the accident. A family friend/photographer was going to take an engagement photograph of me. I drove to the location in an unfamiliar part of Portland, in the rain of course, and had a minor car accident. It was my fault. The other driver got out and started yelling at me. I was scared and started crying, sobbing: "I have to go get my wedding photograph taken." The other driver took pity on me and, after we quickly exchanged insurance information, I somehow made it to the photo shoot. I never liked that picture.

Wedding

Our wedding was March 21, 1970, one week before I turned 21. The day was cool and partly sunny. I wore a white silk, sequined sari. A lovely Indian friend of Jacob's taught me how to drape the seven yards of fabric and use extra pins for security. The small chapel had stained glass windows and a red carpet. My closest girlfriend, Becky, was my maid of honor, and two other friends were bridesmaids. The story of those friendships speaks volumes about how I lived my life. While Becky and I have stayed good friends all these years, our contacts were very infrequent for many years after my wedding. I was too busy to go to her wedding. The second of my wedding attendants and I have maintained a Christmas card friendship, and the third friend died some years after the wedding, with me never having reached out to her after the wedding. It takes time and effort to maintain friendships. I lacked both. I was the first of my high school and college friends to be married. I don't remember attending any of their weddings. I can justify and explain that I had moved out of state, was very busy, and that air travel wasn't as common then as now. But still…not one wedding? Jacob's attendants were my twin brother and two friends, neither of whom he stayed in touch with. We also lost touch with the lovely Indian family—the woman who helped me with the sari.

We had a simple Catholic wedding. The one Indian custom incorporated into the ceremony was the gifting to me of a gold necklace adorned with a tiny beaded cross. This unique piece is called a tali and carries the symbolism of a wedding ring; its gifting is a significant part of the public ritual in an Indian Orthodox wedding in Kerala, India. I came to treasure my tali. It identified me as a Kerala bride. I could recognize other women from Kerala wearing the same piece of jewelry. It made me feel connected. Years later this treasure would come to a violent end when it was yanked off my neck by a thief when I was standing in a crowd watching a parade.

A cake-and-punch reception at the church hall followed the wedding. The guests numbered eighty to ninety, family and friends—but some key people were missing. My grandparents had already died. My aunt and uncle who lived in Portland were not included because I barely knew them. Jacob's few relatives lived far away, and none were present.

My mom wanted to have a dinner celebration right after the wedding for Jacob and me and selected wedding attendees. She proudly planned to bake a fresh Columbia River salmon she and Dad had caught. It grieves me to write that we didn't attend that dinner. Our honeymoon plans were to drive west to the Oregon coast directly after the wedding. Since my parents' home was located in far eastern Portland, this would have taken us way out of our way and likely precluded going to our destination that evening. I made what probably was a feeble pitch to Jacob that we go to the dinner, but quickly was won over to the "practical" plan of leaving directly from the church for our honeymoon. I think back about this episode with much regret, thinking of the pain this must have caused my parents.

Post-Portland

After our honeymoon, Jacob and I moved into an apartment near the medical school in Portland. I completed my requirements for medical school during that semester at Portland State, and Jacob completed his thesis and PhD degree. I was accepted to the University of California, Davis, School of Medicine, where Jacob got a faculty position as an assistant professor at the medical school. That summer of 1970 we set off for California in Jacob's 1964 Dodge Dart, towing a small U-Haul trailer. It never entered my mind that I might be leaving my hometown for good, never again to have Thanksgiving or Christmas with my parents in that city.

Our years at Davis flew by. I studied hard during medical school and graduated in 1974. My memories of medical school are not particularly positive or negative, just blurry. Next came my rotating internship and start of my residency in radiation oncology, both in Sacramento, near Davis. I deliberately chose this specialty because I knew it offered meaningful patient contact, challenging and fascinating pathology, and regular hours. I was always grateful I made this decision.

How can I describe the relationship between Jacob and me during these early years? It was "OK." I was too busy to dwell on our relationship. We enjoyed having a dog. I fondly remember the first night in our first home. We had scant furniture, newspapers covering the windows, and a record playing "Our house is a very, very, very fine house," by Crosby, Stills, Nash & Young. We had a few friends, but no close friends. Occasionally we traveled. I remember a trip to Disneyland in California as fun and a trip to Acapulco, Mexico, as hot.

I recall occasionally being pressured by Jacob to do things I did not want to do. He became very angry once when a male classmate asked me if I wanted to accompany him for an emergency room volunteer opportunity. It sounded interesting and I wanted to go, but backed down because of Jacob's reaction. During a rotation in obstetrics at a satellite hospital, I was encouraged, as were all students, to occasionally stay late or all night to get more labor and delivery experience. Jacob did not like me to stay late. One time I recall coming home early to placate him. I had been expected by the staff to stay, and I really did want to stay until the laboring mother assigned to me delivered her baby. I was reproached by the attending physician the next day. I likely blamed Jacob.

Do you see the pattern? I blamed Jacob when the real problem was that I did not stand up to him and assert myself. We also started to have disagreements about house cleaning, cooking, and laundry. It wasn't his custom to do these tasks, so I just did them. I complained about this injustice, but I gave in and did the work. The ground was cracking to create what would be a long-standing fault line in our marriage.

Oddly, I don't remember feeling lonely during these years—maybe I was too busy for that. I had several friends among the seven women in my class of fifty-two, though we never did anything together, and only one have I kept in touch with. I did not take time for prayer, but I recall occasionally going to the Catholic church in Davis for Mass and even seeing the priest a couple of times about stresses in my marriage.

The Border

Jacob was an excellent teacher. He even received a teacher-of-the-year award. However, his long-standing desire to go to medical school had grown more intense. He applied to and was accepted into an accelerated MD program for PhDs, located in Juarez, Mexico. I understood how important this was for him and agreed to the move. In 1976, right after I completed my second year of post-medical school training, we relocated to El Paso, Texas, which was directly across the border from Juarez. I was able to find a job functioning as an assistant radiation oncologist in a cancer treatment center in El Paso.

The whole El Paso move created a major falling-out between Jacob and my parents, particularly my mom. Once again I was placed between my husband's wishes and that of my parents. At issue was his privacy and wish to keep his matriculation to that particular Mexican school a private matter. I think he was embarrassed to be attending a "foreign" medical school and would have been more open had he been accepted at an American medical school. He was well aware that some medical professionals demean FMGs (foreign medical graduates). My mom wanted to know why I had interrupted my residency and moved rather abruptly to El Paso. At the time I felt that it was unreasonable for him to expect me not to tell my parents why we suddenly moved. But I grudgingly agreed to my husband's wishes and did not give my mom a direct answer—at least not for years. This episode was extremely hurtful to Mom and distressing to me. She repeatedly asked me to tell her what he was doing, why we had moved so suddenly, if we were hiding something? I offered confusing responses about his job or school arrangements, but evaded the truth. Mom was so desperate to know she even made some phone inquiries to El Paso schools seeking information about Jacob. He found out and regarded her probing as proof that she was an intrusive, meddlesome nuisance. I was bombarded by both sides. When he ranted about her to me, I defended her, and thus secured my position in a painful relationship triangle that festered for years.

I eventually came to understand how deeply my husband's family valued appearance, standing in the community, and reputation. Secrets were sometimes necessary to maintain the appearance. But when I look back at this episode, I still shudder. How could I have handled it better? I could have clearly expressed to my husband that I felt his request was unreasonable, and I would not be able to comply. Period. Or, I could have just told my mother that I had decided to respect my husband's desire for privacy about his activities in El Paso. After all, we had been married six years at the time we moved to Texas. Both of these alternatives would have required me to be more honest and clear in my communication and to accept whatever discomfort resulted.

Family Life

The end of our one-year stay in El Paso was marked by a very special event: the birth of our first child, Serena. I was 28 years old. Jacob was 38. We took longer than we had hoped to conceive and were thrilled to be parents. As it turned out, my due date was very close to the time Jacob was to start his first clinical rotation in Chicago, where he would be spending one year doing the hospital clerkships that were part of his medical school curriculum. We did some really dumb things trying to make it possible for him to be present for the birth. First, we asked my El Paso obstetrician for an induction of labor so the baby would come just a little bit earlier. This required first checking the size of the baby compared to the size of my pelvis to be sure the baby could fit through the birth canal. At that time they still used regular X-rays to visualize the baby within the pelvic cavity. Yes, an X-ray. I still have that large X-ray film that features my pelvis and my baby. As you probably know, now we take great pains to avoid exposing fetuses to radiation—fortunately, the risk is much lower with a full-term baby. The doctor concluded that an induction of labor would be possible. But the induction failed. I was still pregnant, and it was time to leave El Paso. Plan B was for Jacob to drive from Texas to Chicago and then two days later for me to fly to Chicago, meet him, and we would then have our baby in Chicago. After he left for Chicago, I stayed in the home of the El Paso doctor I was working with. That night I promptly went into labor. Serena was born early the next morning, without her father being present. She was healthy, beautiful, and ready to nurse. I had never even seen a nursing mother up close and was amazed that she knew what to do.

Chicago

It was early September 1977 when I landed at O'Hare Airport with my one-week-old baby and introduced her to her father. We moved into the Hyde Park neighborhood of Chicago. This was a huge life change. We were new parents. We were new to urban life. I had never seen, much less lived in, a city with such a dense and diverse population. This foreign place measured snow in feet, not inches. Winter was long and dark. We hired our first babysitter, a lovely young mom in our building. We started our new positions, me as a radiation oncology resident and my husband as a medical student in his clerkship year, both at the University of Chicago.

That fall marked the beginning of many hectic years as a working mother. I recall how I constantly carried my baby in my navy blue corduroy belly-pack while cooking, doing housework, or studying. Time passed quickly. I completed the residency and joined what was then called Rush-Presbyterian-St. Luke's Medical Center, with its top-notch day-care center. I learned to juggle an increasing number of balls. My husband was not a partner in childcare or housework. Diapers, baths, and burping were not his thing. Knowing that he had grown up in India, where only women and servants did these tasks, did not make it OK. How could he not see that I was exhausted?

Jacob completed his clerkships and received his long-sought medical degree, achieving this landmark when he was almost forty. We moved to a lovely home in the nearby suburb of Oak Park, Illinois. We were blessed with our second daughter, Sophia.

Life moved on. We had a decent physical relationship, but otherwise our marriage was difficult. He would give me the silent treatment when he was upset with me. I recall one time when I wanted to take the children to Portland to visit my parents. He was adamantly opposed to this long trip as being "unsafe." I went anyway, only to return home to a heavy and enduring silence that lasted for weeks. Sometimes when this happened I just kept talking to him in a one-way, semi-normal tone. But other times I argued or yelled at him trying to get him to talk with me.

In between the relationship blowups, we soldiered on, enjoying our children and some good times. We had a wonderful woman who came to our home each day to help with the children. The children had playmates in the neighborhood, and we occasionally enjoyed Sunday brunches with neighbors. My specialties were bread pudding with orange sauce or a baked cheese blintz/sour cream delight.

Life with young children during long, snowy winters was very challenging. It seemed like each child required seventeen different items of clothing and gear in order to safely go outside in the frigid weather. Hauling these bundled children through the snow to swimming lessons each Saturday at the Y sounds so ludicrous that I can't believe I did it. We lived in the Chicago area during some of the worst winters on record. Snowfall was eighty inches in 1978-79 and seventy-one inches in 1977-78. Our last Chicago winter in 1981-82 brought multiple storms and bitter cold—it was during this winter that our third daughter, Leah, was born.

During these years in the Chicago area, I went to Mass once in a while. I never joined a parish, but I again sought marriage counseling with the priest at a nearby Catholic Church. The priest had no answers for me. He listened with a noncommittal sad face, we prayed, and I trudged back into the cold. Our first two daughters were baptized, neither in a Catholic Church. Sophia actually was baptized by her uncle. My husband's brother-in-law was a Methodist minister; he and his family came to Chicago for a rare family visit and the baptism. Jacob's sister was much older, and I only met her two or three times before she died.

Because I usually just worked in the hospital Monday through Friday and only rarely evenings or weekends, I did have time to myself, especially during the first winters when Jacob was spending more time in the hospital. I started making all types of exotic homemade breads, including a scrumptious sourdough pumpernickel loaf. This hobby filled all kinds of needs: vigorously pounding and kneading the bread, for fun or to vent my frustrations; feeling comforted by the warmth of the kitchen, which was such a contrast to the wind and ice outside; enjoying the pleasure of smelling the bread as it baked. Other than studying medical literature, I didn't read anything. I had few female friends, only one with whom I felt close. She also was a doctor and neither of us had time for each other. Jacob and I had no couple friends. Looking back on these years, I wonder if I was afraid to admit to my unhappiness because then I would have had to face the problems.

The winter of 1981-82 was our last in Illinois. Serena was four, Sophia was two, and we also had our newborn, Leah. We had been married for eleven-and-a-half years. My career path was straightforward. I was a board-certified radiation oncologist with two years of experience as faculty in a medical school. Jacob had a PhD and an MD degree and was sorting out his career options as we prepared to leave Chicago.

Looking Back

Thinking about these years makes me feel sad and confused. Why is it so hard for me to remember details? Had I suppressed experiences or merely been so preoccupied with my work that it precluded a memorable experience of the people and life around me?

It's also hard to comprehend how little I valued myself and how little agency I exercised in my marriage. Remember how I said that my mom "just went along to get along" with my dad? I did the same thing, chronically swallowing my anger and resentment and learning to numb myself to my pain. I thought I was doing the right thing.

I had no support system. My faith was weak. So I did what I always did—I just kept on working hard and hoping for the best.

4

Postcard Perfect

We left behind the bitter cold and snow in Chicago to settle in St. Petersburg, Florida. My job was serving as medical director of a small, new radiation oncology center. I greatly enjoyed working full-time at this hospital-based center. I loved my patients, staff, and colleagues. I had my own office complete with spacious desk, burgundy love seat, mauve desk chair, and a large print of a great blue heron in a rose-silver frame—all carefully selected by me. The only technology was a phone and a dictating machine. The office was my sanctuary.

My husband worked as a doctor in various capacities, at the Veterans Administration, and later in medical business ventures. He was very interested in business and the stock market, which led to great success in managing our personal finances and investments.

We were excited to finally be settling down in Florida, but we just couldn't decide where to live. We rented two successive bayside homes and then bought a ranch house on two-and-a-half acres just outside of St. Petersburg. It was run down with a dirt front yard, no driveway, a tall encircling chain-link fence, two garages overflowing with junk and farm equipment, a swimming pool in which a cow was rumored to have drowned, forest and fields peppered with kennels and cages, and, best of all, three ponies, two goats, and a cage of rabbits. The previous owner was a hermit. Our plan to rebuild the house into a country estate was undone by the large condominium that soon sprung up next to our property. We ended up living on that property, "as is," for two-and-a-half years.

The girls loved playing outside with the animals and cages. Their faces were always smiling and dirty. One time when the girls and I were swimming in the pool, Serena abruptly stood up and shouted, "Listen!" She then led us through the trees where we all witnessed the entire birth of a baby goat, including the mother eating the placenta. Sometimes the animals would escape. All working moms know about the hectic morning rush to get out of the house on time with the children, lunches, bags, projects, etc. I didn't ever dream the morning rush would include having to scale the six-foot, chain-link fence (wearing straight skirt, hose, and heels) to get the goat, which had somehow managed to get into the vacant property next door. Another morning the girls and I had to chase one of the ponies down our dirt road after he had escaped .

The ponies were the miniature variety, but we were still able to ride them—we always referred to them as horses. Teddy, Promise and Jenny were their names. Promise became pregnant. She delivered her foal in the early morning, so we awoke to the miracle of a newborn foal. I still tear up thinking about Star…long legs, wobbly, delicate, soft, new baby smell, and so eager to nuzzle her mamma's udder. She had a white star on her golden tan forehead.

There is one pony story that I am very ashamed to recount. We did not take proper care of our horses. We loved them and fed them, but we didn't arrange veterinary care. We were some combination of ignorant, neglectful, cheap, and oblivious. I wish I could blame my husband. But I was complicit. I could have just stepped up to the need, but I did not. Jenny started looking sick and slowly losing some weight. Then, one day we found her dead in the back pasture area. What do you do with a 600-pound dead pony in your backyard, especially if you are guilty of neglect? Who to call? What to do? We waited until dark, dragged the very heavy horse to a remote area of the property and buried her. I am glad God is merciful and that, if this was a crime, the statute of limitations is expired. I later expressed to my daughters my sincere regret about this incident. We did reform our ways because later that year, when Star was seriously injured, we took her to our wonderful small animal vet. He even kenneled her for several days to better manage her wounds.

Our three girls stayed busy playing with one another or their friends, taking gymnastics and swimming lessons, and participating in school activities. They attended some day care, but more commonly, when they weren't in school, they were home with our housekeeper/babysitter. We always had dogs and cherish our tender memories of Raj and Misty—and, we always did take the dogs to the vet. Raj was a noble, deeply loved German shepherd and Misty was a bean-brained, small, red Doberman famous for her intense frown as she posed to ferociously attack the ever-present Florida lizards.

We moved from the farm into what we thought would be our dream house, a brick home on Boca Ciega Bay in western St. Petersburg. We got really carried away with this house, which we rebuilt from a smaller home. It was a gated mansion with five bedrooms, five baths, an office, a library, and a swimming pool. The home was situated on a large lot with dozens and dozens of palm and oak trees. But we never fully settled in. The empty space story makes this sadly clear. The dining room of our home opened through French doors to the backyard with its pool, trees, and water's edge. One wall was mirrored. A large chandelier hung in the middle of this empty space. My husband and I never could agree on a dining table. For all the years we lived in that house, we had no dining table. We ate at our vinyl upholstered breakfast nook in the family room. The infrequent times we had guests, we used a folding table to extend the nook. We used the empty space only one time, for a work-related affair, for which we rented a table. As I visualize that empty space in my mind, I am stopped short by the juxtaposition of a baby grand piano in the adjacent alcove. This piano was the nicest gift ever given to me by Jacob—when I saw it for the first time I burst into tears. Such were the paradoxes in our home.

First Diagnosis

One warm fall afternoon in 1990 the girls were playing basketball in the front driveway. Eight-year-old Leah had a cold. But why was she so listless? She just sat on the ground, watching her sisters with dull eyes. Then we noticed the tiny red spots and a few bruises. The pediatrician checked her blood and called us that evening. Leah had 3,000 platelets, instead of the usual 300,000. Platelets are the blood element that helps the blood to clot, so we immediately started worrying about serious bleeding complications. After the phone call Jacob and I stood together in our grand mirrored foyer, had a meaningful "we can do this hug," and then set off to meet the pediatric hematologist/oncologist, a colleague, on the second floor of the children's hospital. This was the leukemia unit, the same place where Serena's friend and classmate, Ellie, had suffered and died from leukemia not long before. Leah needed to have a bone marrow sample extracted from her pelvic bone, just like I was sure that Ellie had had done to her. I remember the hollow echoes of the reassurance: "Don't worry. It's probably not leukemia…"

Thank God, it wasn't leukemia, although it was a serious autoimmune illness that required ongoing intravenous infusions. Leah suffered significant side effects from the medications. As the first year slid into the second year, she required treatments less often, but it became obvious that she had a chronic illness. Leah and our family dealt with it, just as so many of my patients routinely dealt with diagnoses far more grim than Leah's. We learned the challenges of parenting a child who is ill. She often did not feel well, was tired and achy. The treatments made her sick. She had to deal with needles and IV lines way more than a youngster should have to. It was hard to know what our expectations for her should be. It was easy to be permissive, perhaps over-permissive, attributing a bad attitude or occasional misbehavior to the illness or the medicines. The frequency of her treatment gradually lessened—initially every day or two, then weekly, gradually to monthly, and finally only occasionally. The infusion of May 1995, five years after diagnosis, ended up being the last for many years. She still needed regular blood checks, but she was stable off all treatment. We took a deep breath of relief.

Relationships

On the surface, I had it made. The kids were doing well and liked their school. Most of the time we had a good baby-sitter and housekeeping help. We had sufficient income. I loved my children. I loved my job. I really think I loved my husband, but it was getting harder. I didn't understand how he could be so uncaring about my exhaustion, especially on Sunday evenings. I frequently made a nice Sunday dinner, sometimes Indian chicken curry with chapatis and cabbage thoran. By the time I cooked, we ate, I cleaned up the mess, and got lunches and everything squared away for Monday, I was beat. The girls helped me, but I did most of the work. All this time Jacob would be upstairs in the TV room watching travel or news shows. For years, I rationalized his lack of help, convincing myself that it was his culture. And, after all, I did have paid help with the housework. So, it would be OK, I thought.

But it wasn't OK. With time, my resentment grew. There were occasional blowups. I remember more than once running from the dinner table in tears, vaulting up the adjacent open staircase, and looking down on the frightened faces of my girls and the angry face of my husband, all watching me flee. I cannot clearly recall the details of these fights, but the explosions usually related to a defense of myself, the girls, or my mom about something Jacob was saying.

My mom and dad came to visit a few times and the girls and I also visited Portland several times, but it always provoked a huge fight about something that was said or not said. My mom would cry on the phone to me, "He is the only person in the world I have ever known who doesn't like me." Jacob had specific complaints, such as the car insurance he had to pay for in 1969 or the lack of hospitality he perceived at a lunch at my family home in 1970. That second incident is telling. My mom took pride in serving just the right amount of food, since she didn't have storage space and didn't want to waste. These moderate servings turned that meal into an insult for Jacob, accustomed as he was to the typical huge spread traditionally offered in India. He also felt my mom was "nosy," as evidenced by her efforts to try to find out why we had so mysteriously moved to Texas in 1976. I devalued his complaints and often defended my mom, strengthening the pernicious triangle between him, her and myself. Mom always mailed Christmas presents to all of us. One year she sent him a box of macadamia nuts. As we sat under the tree, he opened this gift and disdainfully tossed it to the ground, spilling the nuts to mix with the colored ribbons and wrapping paper strewn around. Christmas was always a challenge for me because I had so much to do: decorations, food, gift shopping and wrapping, and Christmas stockings—usually without too much time off work.

My father had been doing well on kidney dialysis for a number of years, but eventually his health started failing. In 1989 he made the decision to stop the dialysis, knowing that meant he would die within days or weeks. I joined the rest of the family in Oregon for what was a good-bye reunion for Dad. He was secure with his decision, told me he had made peace with God, and greatly enjoyed the family time. I had made coverage arrangements for my practice. The babysitter and Jacob would be handling things at home. Dad's condition remained stable for the first week. I was so confused about how long I should or could stay in Portland. What about the kids? What about my practice? After ten days I finally decided to return to Florida. It was a tearful good-bye. Dad died comfortably at home a few days later, with my mom and my sister-in-law in attendance.

I look back with horror, shame, and sadness about my decision not to return to Portland for my father's funeral. I told myself that I was with Dad when it counted. I didn't think of the irreplaceable role I should have played to support my mom. It was only after I was widowed myself that I realized how unfeeling and callous my decision had been. I don't fully understand why I made that choice. Maybe Jacob discouraged me from returning. I know I worried about the kids, my patients, and the substitute doctor. I also fretted that the hospital administration might think I wasn't adequately fulfilling my contract to provide radiation oncology services at the hospital. This is my list of excuses. I recently attended the funeral for a man who was a neighbor. Watching this man's daughters lovingly tend to their newly widowed mother as they helped her to her seat in the front of church pierced me deeply. My excuses do not lessen my sadness. As I've done many times before, I said a prayer, told Mom I was sorry, thanked God for his abundant forgiveness, and asked for the grace to forgive myself and do better in the future.

Jacob and I also argued about my work. He wanted to be more involved in the financial running of my practice than I wanted him to be. In spite of his business expertise, I did not want him involved because I wanted to preserve my work as a sacrosanct conflict-free zone of my very own. He often challenged me about one doctor with whom I worked, thinking him to be overly friendly to me.

Criticism was common in our home. I cringe when I remember him mocking my hairstyle if I got it cut shorter than he liked. He once took a photo of the back of my neck as I was bending down to look at the paper and mocked my skinny "chicken" neck now exposed because of the haircut. I've tried to remember the ways I criticized him. It is a little shocking to see how clearly I remember his criticisms, and actually all his infractions, but not my own. I know I protested about his lack of help with the house and kids and also told him he was not being fair to my mom. As our three daughters started entering their teen years, we increasingly fought about the best way to parent them, and I know I criticized him about that.

There were good times. We enjoyed many family trips to the nearby beaches and parks, as well as lovely vacations. The long days picnicking under the Australian pines on the beach in Anna Maria Island near Bradenton standout as special memories. We vacationed at Cape Canaveral and Miami and went on several Caribbean cruises. Starting in middle school, the girls enjoyed sports—as they got older they concentrated on volleyball—at which they all excelled. It was fun for us. The sad fact is that, for me, the negative memories overshadow the positive ones. This is probably due to the fact that any memory born in a bed of negative emotions, like anger or shame, will be retained longer and more vividly than a positive memory. That's just the way the brain works.

Awareness

I finally started admitting the depth of my unhappiness, looking in self-help books to find answers. I hadn't read anything other than medical literature for years. It is impossible to overstate how much I learned and grew from my reading that started during these years. I pored over the pages and devoured the words and quotes. I started to accumulate quotes, readings, and, later, prayers and meditations and kept them in a special box. Late at night, when my husband was asleep, I would sit on the floor of our bedroom with my box, crying and reading these words of wisdom.

It was during these years that I first read Scott Peck's *The Road Less Traveled: A New Psychology of Love, Traditional Values and Spiritual Growth*. This book influenced me greatly and is the first book I read multiple times. Peck, a psychiatrist, writes about "using discipline to solve life's problems"—to deal with pain and suffering in ways that help us learn and grow. His four discipline tools or "techniques of suffering"[3] are honesty, delayed gratification, personal responsibility, and balance. He says these tools are not complex, but we must have the will to use the tools and this will is driven by love. I did a self-evaluation of my earlier years. Here is my pass-fail scorecard on these four points:

1. Honesty-fail. I wasn't honest with myself.

2. Delayed gratification-pass. In my work and study life, I was very good at delaying gratification.

3. Accepting personal responsibility-fail. I now realize that instead of taking responsibility for my decisions, I often blamed others, especially Jacob.

4. Balance-fail. I just kept on working and ignored my inner needs and needs of loved ones. I did not love myself enough to deal with the conflict I might face if I stood up for myself.

---

3. Scott Peck, *The Road Less Traveled* (Simon and Schuster, 1978), 17-18.

The problem was, of course, that these patterns of behavior became so deeply entrenched over the years that I was hardly aware of them. But I was beginning to see some cracks in those hardened patterns.

I remember feeling a deep pit in my stomach when I finally started to realize that I could not change my husband. I had dwelled on his issues and behaviors for years. It took a long time for me to fully accept the painful reality that I could only change myself. It sounds obvious, but when you are locked in a difficult relationship, it is not. I think many or most individuals who divorce blame the divorce on their partner's inability or unwillingness to change themselves for the better.

Reading Harriet Lerner's *Dance of Anger*[4] helped me understand that I might face negative consequences as I started to change myself. Over the years, Jacob and I had developed our own dance routine, unhealthy as it was. Now I was changing my dance step. Unless he changed his dance step, he would step on my feet or we might even fall down—unless I changed back to my old step.

I yearned to spend time with a couple of women friends, but always felt guilty taking time away from the children to do things for myself. I would tell myself that I was already away from them enough because of my work. I agonized over this issue, but finally began occasionally going to early breakfast with female friends. I would be super organized at home so I could meet my friend at 7:30 a.m. at Bob Evans or Copper Kitchen. We would talk nonstop until we rushed off to work around 9—late. This was invigorating. It felt like I had stepped out of a dark and musty room onto a beach with sunshine and a fragrant breeze. I inhaled deeply as

4. Harriet Lerner, *Dance of Anger* (Harper and Row, 1985).

I savored the healing bond between women friends who listen and share from the heart. Once this door had been opened, I flung open the house. I thought about all my women acquaintances: mothers of other children, teachers, or colleagues from work. "They would make great friends," I told myself, if only I ever took the time to be friends. So, I drafted and typed up a no-frill invitation to these women, telling them I needed friends and inviting them to my first "Ladies' Party." I offered a format for sharing and asked each one to bring some creation that they had made or valued. About ten women came that first night and did we ever talk and laugh. My daughters were flabbergasted at the racket and "cachinations" (their description) and said my laugh was the loudest. The gatherings continued for a year or two and eventually morphed into a book club.

As for my physical health, I still didn't pay too much attention. In school I hadn't played sports, and as an adult I didn't get much exercise. It caught up with me in my forties when my back started hurting from arthritis and being out of shape. I was given back exercises by the orthopedist and started an intermittent program at home, but still did not begin a regular exercise routine. That would have to wait a couple of decades.

Buds of Faith

Though my personal study and my growing friendships helped me tremendously, I still felt restless and unhappy. Maybe this is the feeling St. Augustine describes in *Confessions* when he says to God, "I am restless until I rest with Thee." I started to think more about God and wanted to figure out what my faith was all about. Did I really believe in God? What about Jesus? Did I believe Jesus died for me?

Did having faith come with any obligations? I was raised as a Christian and had drifted away from church because of busyness rather than a clear decision to do so. Was I still a Christian? Why wasn't I going to church? What about the children, who only sporadically had attended church services? While I am not sure of the sequence or exact timing of my faith journey during these years, I am crystal clear about some of the details. I know I carefully studied the book *Mere Christianity,* a classic by C.S. Lewis. I liked his form of apologetics…an intellectual approach that led to his own conversion and helped me get a better grip on the mystery of faith. He asks and explains hard questions…like how Christ's death somehow puts us right with God.[5]

Somewhere along the line I discovered the amazing fact that faith is a decision…it is not some powerful wave of emotion that overcomes an unsuspecting unbeliever. The *Catechism of the Catholic Church*[6] states that faith is a grace, a gift, but we must decide whether to accept this gift. My logic told me that there has to be a God. The awesome human body and the whole of creation are not an accident. The human mind with its ability to love, think, and be creative could not be just a fleeting existence to no end, no purpose. Yes, I knew that I did believe in a loving Creator God. So, finally, I said yes to God. "I accept your gift of faith." I also decided I believed that Jesus Christ was the Son of God and my Redeemer, basing this conclusion on history, the Bible, writings of holy men and women over the years, and tradition. My adult spiritual life had begun, leading me to study, prayer, reading the entire Bible, and eventually returning to church.

5. C. S. Lewis, *Mere Christianity*, p. 57
6. *Catechism of the Catholic Church* (Liguori Publications, 1994), 41.

Returning to church, however, wasn't so straightforward. Initially I was reluctant to return to my childhood faith of Catholicism. I didn't want to embrace all those rules again, especially if it would mean feeling guilty all the time, like I used to feel. I was not a big sinner. I was a normal kid, a little sinner. But the childhood faith that I had absorbed did not come with joy, gratitude, and trust in a loving and gentle God. I realized that the faith of my youth had become tainted with scrupulosity and pharisaism. So, I looked elsewhere. Since we all respected the Salvation Army ministry, the children and I went there next. The church was unique with its brass band and uniformed officers, but it just didn't feel right. Next we tried the Methodist Church. The folks there were very welcoming, maybe too welcoming—I felt a little uncomfortable, like how it felt when someone stands too close to you to talk. The Lutheran Church was next. It was comfortable and familiar. I was thrilled to learn that Dr. Edward Weiss and his wife were active in this parish. Ed was a medical oncologist whom I greatly respected—he and I worked together regularly. After attending this Lutheran Church for several months, I decided to enroll the children in its Sunday School. That is when my husband (who had been raised in the Catholic- influenced Mar Thoma Church in India) intervened. He protested, "Even the Catholic Church is better than the Lutheran Church." He had not been a part of the search committee, but, nonetheless, something made me listen to him. Maybe that "something" was my continuing inability to confront and disagree with him, but maybe it was a weird way for God to call me back to Catholicism.

On Thanksgiving Day, 1989, I took the children to Mass at the nearby Catholic Church. It turned out to be an extraordinary experience. It felt like coming home, like returning to your family Thanksgiving table after many years away. I got warm and felt tears come. The music, the liturgy, the smell of candles, the lines of people receiving Communion, the times of hushed silence—it was all so comfortable. Of course, it was new to the children, now age seven, nine, and twelve. They didn't much like CCD, the religious education classes, in which I eventually enrolled them. With time I was joyfully able to return to the sacraments. The director of religious education was an enthusiastic, God-filled, happy woman who steered me into a Bible study, which took place during the children's classes. We sat in a circle around a candle listening to "Your light is a lamp unto my feet." Every time I hear Amy Grant singing that song I am carried back to that room. I became very close friends with two of the women in the Bible study group. What a joyous time this was for me as I started anew on my spiritual journey, trying to be wide open to God's will for me. I felt profound gratitude realizing that my God and the church had just been waiting for me all those years, ready to welcome me back with open arms. I guess this is how the prodigal son felt upon his return home.

Planning for the girls to officially join the Catholic Church created yet another rift between Jacob and me. You see, the youngest, Leah, had never been baptized, and this was required so she could attend religious education with her class for First Communion preparation. The church prescribed that this must take place inside the church building. Jacob was opposed to this, as he wanted her baptized at home, like the others had been. He was adamant. The priest was adamant. That left me sobbing in the middle. I recall sitting in the rectory office loudly wailing to the priest, "What do you want me to do? Leave my husband so my daughter can be baptized?" This tearful stalemate went on for months until my husband shocked me by withdrawing his opposition. This was a dramatic and unexpected capitulation; I was very grateful and relieved. He even came to the church service when they were all officially brought into the church. I am embarrassed to say that my memories of that sacred celebration center on the flowered wreaths with chiffon veils that I had made for them and on the swim party at our home afterward.

The Future

The girls were busy and most of the time seemed to be happy. I was celebrating my renewed faith and return to the Catholic Church. My radiation oncology medical practice gave me great satisfaction. I had started reading again and enjoyed some close women friends. When I watched the sunset from our dock I felt that all was well: the water shimmered, the salty air smelled robust, and the brown pelicans dive-bombed for a late dinner. It was hard to imagine the storms that lay over the horizon.

Looking Back

These years were marked by work, worry, and questions. I worked hard, as always. I worried about my children. I wondered why I couldn't make things better and why there was so much pain in our marriage when Jacob and I did love each other, which is what I believed. I also wondered or, more accurately, feared how Jacob would respond to the changes I was starting to make. I especially wondered what God wanted me to do.

These were very hard years. I hurt, and I'm pretty sure that Jacob suffered just as much as I did. Our children could not be shielded from the dysfunction in our relationship. The good news is that my pain had finally driven me to start making some changes, the biggest being letting God back into my life.

5

Abraham Experience

Everyone in the lab at my hospital knew me. The Radiation Oncology Center, where I worked, was just around the corner from the lab. I was a regular, stopping in to review the pathology slides on my patients or to drop off Leah's blood samples that I had been bringing in from home since her diagnosis in 1990. One morning in the summer of 1994, Jacob asked me to take a sample of his blood to the lab. He looked and acted tired, but wouldn't say much—only that he didn't feel well. I still worried that he was depressed. He sat around for hours watching news and documentaries. Using the supplies I had on hand from Leah's care, I obtained Jacob's blood sample that morning and dropped it at the lab. His cell counts were almost normal, but when the pathologist looked at the blood sample under the microscope he found a few cells that didn't appear quite normal. There was no diagnosis, but the pathologist recommended follow-up blood tests just to be sure all was OK.

During the months that followed, I intermittently took Jacob's blood to the lab. I would sit at a microscope with the pathologist and peer at the blood cells on the slides. Gradually the samples began to contain more abnormal cells. In June 1995, which was one year after his first blood test and exactly one month after what turned out to be Leah's last intravenous infusion for many years, Jacob underwent a bone marrow biopsy by a hematology-oncology specialist. This is a painful procedure in which a large needle is inserted through the back pelvic bone in order to suck out a sample of bone marrow. The result confirmed the fears of the pathologist. Jacob had a serious blood disorder. The diagnosis was myelodysplasia, which is a spectrum of precancerous and cancerous disorders caused by abnormal cells being produced in the bone marrow. He and I went to a university specialty center for consultation. Particularly back then, there was no consensus on how to manage myelodysplasia. Jacob's case was not felt to be the aggressive type. Sometimes patients with his kind of problem could live a long time, as with a chronic disease. The experts offered two alternatives: different types of chemotherapy or close observation. There were no good studies, and the doctors were not enthusiastic about what the chemotherapy might offer. I couldn't draw on any professional experience with myelodysplasia as I did not treat patients with this disease. We talked, and Jacob chose the close observation option. It was very confusing. Looking back, I don't think we fully grasped the potential seriousness of the diagnosis.

Another Diagnosis

During the spring of Serena's senior year in high school in 1995, a few months before Jacob's biopsy, while I was cleaning up after dinner and Jacob was upstairs watching the news, Serena was entertaining her boyfriend, Mike. Mike came in the kitchen, with an uncharacteristically somber expression, and quietly asked me to come to the library. I followed him to where Serena was slumped over on the couch. Serena had assigned him the task of informing me that she had an eating disorder, had suffered from it for three years, and was desperate to get help. My stomach tightened. It had never entered my mind, even for a second, that Serena was suffering from an eating disorder. Certainly I was aware of problems, just not that one.

Serena and her sisters had blossomed into beautiful teenagers who were very American. Their father's ideas of appropriate dress and activities were very different from theirs. My ideas were somewhere in between. The result of these differences was conflict and pain in our family. Jacob didn't trust the girls and their friends. He sometimes spoke to them in ways that sounded disrespectful and mocking. I would defend the girls and try to soften the rules. He would try to tighten up the restrictions to counteract my leniency. The girls were top students, excelled in sports, and had wonderful friends. If you overheard the cross-examinations in our home, you might have thought they were flunking out, skipping school, or hiding drug habits. Jacob was hypervigilant about boys. He was certain that all they wanted was to have sex with his daughters. Maybe he was right. I wasn't as available and open to my daughters as I should have been, especially on this subject. I grew up in a family that was tight-lipped about sex and sensuality, and I only had sex with one man, my husband. I did have the perfunctory talk about reproduction, talked a little about sex, and saw to it that the girls visited a gynecologist as teens. I deeply regret I did not try to engage them in an honest and intimate conversation on the subject.

I know that Jacob's words and actions stemmed from love, but somehow it was a love distorted by fear. He had an urgent need to know everything and control the girls in order to protect them from harm. Conflicts about dress, boys, dating, parties, drinking, and curfews became the norm in our family. I shudder when I think about the toxic lack of trust and respect that they experienced. Serena and Sophia, as the two older sisters, were most affected by what I eventually understood was an intensely shaming environment. Only gradually did I come to realize the confusion, guilt, and humiliation they no doubt experienced just for having normal teenage desires to be with their friends and be like their friends. I think I buried the painful details: the interrogations of the girls, the eavesdropping on the phone, the grilling of their friends, or Jacob's violent ripping of the MC Hammer poster off Sophia's bedroom wall. Even though I knew things were hard for the girls, I recognize now that I didn't fully appreciate how bad they really were. I even thought Leah, the youngest, had been spared—until years later when she told me of a painful event that took place when she was in third grade. She had been entrusted to hold onto a note written by a girl to another boy, and it was still in her pocket when she came home from school. She was very afraid her dad would find it. She couldn't stop thinking about it and described, "It felt like it was burning a hole in my pocket." She thought that a note for a boy, if discovered, would provoke a loud, angry response from her father. To avoid this, she tore the small note into "five thousand pieces" and snuck out to the dumpster by the street to deposit them where her dad would never find them. She vividly recalls how scared she was, how desperate to be rid of the evidence, and how hard her heart was pounding.

I cry when I relive the strife in our home. Our marriage was shaken to its foundation by the constant disagreements and harsh tone. When I stood up for the girls, it only made Jacob double down. I did nothing to facilitate healing in our family. Was it that I didn't know what to do? Or was I afraid of what would happen if I took a strong stand? It was as though I was paralyzed. I had no understanding that I was as emotionally unavailable to my girls as my mom had been to me. It is so sad to think about me, Jacob, and my mom—all of us who tried very hard to love, yet were so off track.

If Jacob were to write a memoir, what would he say about all of this? I think he would write about his precious daughters and how much he loved them and wanted to protect them. I really don't know what he would say about me. Maybe that I took the girls' side to curry their favor, to win their love. Maybe that I just didn't care enough or wasn't brave enough to say what needed to be said to keep them safe. Maybe that I backed my mom more than him because I loved her more. Maybe that I always just did and said what was required for people to think I was nice. I read these suppositions and wonder if they contain kernels of truth.

With this family story, it is not surprising that Serena developed an eating disorder. I was deeply saddened to know she suffered alone for three years and that I had no idea. Not a hint. I informed Jacob who, of course, was deeply concerned. He and I together jumped into action mode to find what we thought was the best treatment for her, an outpatient therapist, whom Serena saw regularly for a while. I was never sure how she was doing, but with the input of the therapist, we made a joint decision that she would be ready to start college in the fall as originally had been planned. Jacob and I drove her the 150 miles to the University of Florida in Gainesville and helped her get situated in the dorm, including the traditional trip to Walmart to buy supplies, and the last dinner together. She seemed fine, but wasn't as ready as we had thought. She ended up taking a leave of absence from school later in the fall semester for a four-week inpatient intensive treatment program. Family counseling was recommended as part of her therapy, but as I recall, this only lasted for one or two sessions. Jacob didn't think that family or parenting issues had anything to do with Serena's problem. I was convinced then and now that family and parenting issues had everything to do with the diagnosis. A recent list of the factors that contribute to the development of eating disorders starts with genetics, followed by family distress, described as "families with high perceived parental expectations for achievement and appearance, families who communicate poorly, have members who are enmeshed with or estranged from each other, devalue the mother or the maternal role, have marital tension, or have difficulties managing conflict."[7] We certainly fit this description, including my past history of an eating disorder.

Christmas 1995 came and went. I think as a family we were treading water, afraid to try any new strokes or reach out for help for fear we might sink or even drown.

Marriage in Decline

During these years my emotions were all over the place. Depending on the day or week, I might feel desperate, angry, sad, resolute, confused or, most commonly, numb. I was afraid for my girls, for my marriage, for me, and for my

7. UpToDate, Topic 2093 Version 36.0

husband. Looking back at this whirlwind of emotions, it is hard to outline the precise sequence of events. But many details are painfully clear.

Over the years, Jacob and I had developed recurring unhealthy patterns of relating to each other. I would become more strident as I tried to talk with him and get him to respond. In turn, he would regress further inside himself, except for the outbursts. I received "silent treatments" intermittently throughout our marriage—infrequent, unpredictable, and lasting days, weeks, and one time nearly three months. I think that most of the time I responded by ignoring the silence and pretending it wasn't happening, except when it would become so oppressive that I would lash out. I thought if I maintained a civil and conversational tone, maybe the girls wouldn't notice it was a unidirectional conversation. We continued to have intermittent big fights, like the confrontation about the New Mexico trip that had happened five years earlier.

Now I was reading more books about communication, marriages, and faith. I desperately needed answers to my questions. What should I do? What did God want me to do? There was one Christian book about marriage, the name which I cannot recall, that particularly provoked me. It purported you could always save your marriage, even if you were the only one in the marriage doing the loving.

I reached out for help, first to my pastor. This further upset my husband, who was incensed I would share personal details with a priest—a priest who might even be part of the priest scandal so prominent in the news even back then. As it turned out, that pastor was arrested a few years later and convicted of sexual abuse of children. I saw a psychiatrist and later a therapist and finally convinced Jacob to go with me—but he only would go a couple of times. The therapist stressed healthy communication and concentrating on our own feelings and experiences, not those of our spouse. This was very challenging for us.

I secretly visited a divorce attorney hoping we could get a legal separation. This seemed like a plausible solution, maybe just to give us a temporary respite. But I learned there was no such thing as a legal separation in Florida.

In the midst of all this, Jacob amazingly agreed to go with me to a Retrouvaille Retreat. Retrouvaille is like a Christian marriage encounter weekend, except it is designed for seriously challenged marriages on the verge of breakup. I saw this as a lifeline. We went and participated. We prayed together. Couples shared their stories of loss and redemption. Jacob did not want to attend the follow-up group sessions, but I was still so grateful and so hopeful. He actually liked and respected the small, smiley priest who was in charge. We went to visit him several times for counseling, and he even came to our home. But over the following months we fell back into our same destructive patterns. Why is it so often like this in relationships? I knew he was very unhappy. I often thought, and still do, that he was seriously depressed. I didn't know what to do for him or our marriage. Things I did for me (such as returning to church, visiting family, developing friendships) helped me, but did not help our marriage. In fact, they just seemed to increase the space between us.

Somewhere during this painful journey I returned to the divorce attorney. My worries about my daughters had become unbearable. Serena was a high school senior, Sophia a sophomore, and Leah in eighth grade. I loved them so much. It was excruciating to know that I was a major player in our family turmoil. At the lawyer's recommendation, I started surreptitiously copying investment and banking records from Jacob's home office and sneaking them off to my office in the hospital, where I had a secret file. I would be flooded with sickening waves of disloyalty and guilt as I did this—over and over, bit by bit. Over time I created a fat file, which I kept securely locked up.

By this time, Jacob and I had mentioned divorce during some of our angry rows. He would become very loud and threaten to take the girls. He claimed he would get a lawyer and fight me at every step. I can still visualize him standing in our bedroom, his face so hard, as he hollered at me about taking the girls. I was afraid. I had decided to get a divorce, but was procrastinating. I have pondered long and hard as to why I was resistant. Did I feel that my marriage was God-ordained and, hence, permanent? Was it good old-fashioned Catholic guilt? Was it shame? Was I trying to avoid a personal failure, which I perceived divorce to be? Was it the social stigma? Was I afraid of the battle that it might become? Did I really think he had any grounds to his threat of taking the girls from me? Was I just being realistic in admitting that divorce would not solve our family problems? After all, even after a divorce we would still somehow need to parent our daughters. I was not concerned about financial insecurity after divorce, a worry that many women share. I had been the majority breadwinner for many years, having landed in one of the more lucrative specialties in medicine. I do not think his illness influenced my thinking about divorce one way or the other—our relationship had deteriorated long before his diagnosis of myelodysplasia. I have absolutely no recollection thinking that I should stall the divorce because he was sick and might die, hence saving me from having to get a divorce. Nor do I remember thinking that I had to stay married because he was sick and would need me.

So why was I unwilling to move ahead with a divorce? I don't know. I have no answer. The end result was that I didn't act. I guess it was less scary to hope that something would change for the better than to act. I decided to just keep trying.

In spite of my fledging connections in the church and new friends, I still felt very alone, even when I prayed. But one time I had an experience that showed me I wasn't alone. It was in the night. Jacob was asleep, on his side of the king-size bed. I was on my side of the bed, drifting between wakefulness and sleep, my mind full of tangled worries. My right arm was stretched out to the side, partially extending off the bed. Then it happened. I felt a gentle hand firmly grasp my hand. I remember getting teary and calmly thinking it must be Jesus. Feeling totally at peace, I drifted back to sleep. This could have been a dream or imagination growing from a desperate need, but I prefer to think that it was the hand of Jesus offering me solace.

Dark Clouds

Time didn't move forward in a normal way during these difficult times. Instead, it was as if the days, years, fights, counselors, lawyers, tears, and lamentations became jumbled together in a maze with no entrance or exit. My experience certainly matches the research showing that traumatic experiences like mine characteristically result in chaotic and disorderly memories that are heavily influenced by the emotional state at the time of the experience.

I find it hard to believe that this escalating marital strife occurred during the same period when Jacob and I were dealing with major health concerns about Leah and Serena, as well as his blood disorder. We didn't know if Leah would require lifetime treatment. Would the experimental infusions she was receiving continue to work? Would Serena permanently recover from her eating disorder? Could she stay in school? Did Jacob have a disease that might require aggressive treatment? I continued to work full time. The girls continued their busy lives.

I prayed with increasing desperation to my God. I begged for a clear answer. What was I supposed to do? Was now the time for the divorce? I didn't hear any answers. I could only see darkness.

Then out of the blue, in 1994 or early 1995, Jacob offered to go to a second Retrouvaille retreat. I was flabbergasted—this offer was totally unexpected. I wondered if this would just further drag out the torture that our marriage had become. But I didn't want to be the one to extinguish what might be the last flicker of hope for our marriage—so we went on the retreat. I don't remember much about it, but it provided an opportunity to pray and think. My heart opened a little, which allowed me to admit that, in the last year or two, Jacob actually had twice before taken totally unexpected conciliatory steps. Once was when he went to the first Retrouvaille Retreat and the other was when he unexpectedly agreed to Leah being baptized in the Catholic Church, after months of absolute refusal to even consider this possibility. Each of these three actions came when I was at the end of my rope, ready to let go of the marriage.

My sudden recognition of his three conciliatory steps jolted me to rapt, upright attention. I took a deep breath. Three times Jacob had acted in totally unexpected ways. Had God prodded him to take these three steps? Was this grace in action? Was God repeatedly trying to tell me something, just like in the First Book of Samuel when he had thrice attempted to get Samuel's attention? I eventually concluded that, yes, God was communicating with me. But I was deeply disturbed. I saw no conversion on Jacob's part, no repentance. Yes, it was good that he had taken these three steps, but our conflicts continued. My reaction may sound paradoxical, but I did not perceive this sign from God as good news. I wanted a new marriage or an exit strategy. This direct grace felt nothing like a gentle breeze from the Holy Spirit. Instead, it felt like a battering storm. Here my memory is very clear. I tighten up remembering how angry I was with God. I had been praying so hard for answers, and finally I had conclusively decided, again, that I would get a divorce. Now it seemed like God would just not leave me alone. Each time I had finally become convinced I was supposed to get a divorce, Jacob had stepped up. It so clearly felt like this was God's way of telling me that he did not want me to get a divorce— that I was supposed to keep trying—that there was reason for hope. I felt that the "Hound of Heaven" from Francis Thompson's 1893 poem was badgering me and telling me I was to stay married. As I've described, by this time in my life I did have a prayer life, so when I finally accepted God's role in all this, I had my rebuttal all ready for Him. "But God, what about the girls? How can you expect them to live in a home like this? I am so frightened for them. I worry that they will be affected by the distrust, disrespect, and awful fighting going on in our home! I don't know what to do! What do you want me to do? I don't want them to be hurt," and on and on.

Standing by the Pit

When I think back on my life up to the present, I find that at no point was I lower than during this interval. I was spent. Jacob was so tired and unhappy. What did his positive steps mean for the future of our marriage? The wild up-and-down cycles were emotionally and physically exhausting. I felt dazed. I did not want to ignore God if he was really trying to tell me something. So I kept on praying, but not with delicate prayers of humble petition. No, I prayed loudly with desperate prayers of loss, pain, worry, and lamentation—mostly alone at night, sometimes with women friends, or at Mass.

Clarity came in a painfully slow process. Eventually God's message to me became clear. I had to surrender to God's will. I could not fix my marriage, but I was to stay married. As for the girls, I was to surrender them to the loving arms of our Almighty God and Savior Jesus Christ. I was to trust God that he would take care of my precious daughters.

So, I let go. I stepped back from the edge of the pit and cried.

I reminded myself over and over that my girls were in good hands. The shocking part of this prayer experience came when I realized that I felt like Abraham must have felt. Abraham was asked to sacrifice his son, Isaac, to God. With profound trust in his loving God, he prepared to do just that. But God stepped in and saved Isaac. I had been asked to surrender Serena, Sophia, and Leah to God's care. Like Abraham, I experienced great anguish in making this commitment to surrender my offspring. The Bible calls it a sacrifice. That is how it felt. And that is how it still feels. Afterward, I felt more peace than I had for a very long time.

I felt certain I was doing the right thing. To this day, if I ever find myself worrying about my daughters, I remember my "Abraham experience" and feel a renewed trust in our loving God, into whose arms I surrendered my marriage and my daughters so long ago.

Some might say: "She never heard God. She just made that up because she didn't have the courage to get a divorce, which she clearly should have done." I have asked myself that same question. All I can say is that at the time I just knew. I had no doubt. It was crystal clear that God wanted me to stay married. Somehow he would help Jacob and me, and, as I explained, he would especially shepherd my daughters.

I told Jacob that I was not going to pursue a divorce. The strain between us eased. It was like the pressure valve had been released on the pressure cooker that was our marriage—so an explosion was no longer possible. I took a few easy breaths. Life went on.

Looking Back

Living through these difficult years gave me intense empathy for all those in troubled marriages and for those who end up getting divorced. Marital discord is a painful trauma for the couple and for the children in the family. In my life it has been the greatest trauma. Later in my life I would come to better understand what happened and see many things I wished I had done differently during these years. But we can only live our lives in a forward direction. I only hope that what I learned and share in this book will help you move forward with self-knowledge and emotional health—so you can avoid your own relationship pit or find your path out of it more quickly than I did.

I now see that this dark time was the turning point in my relationship with God—although it felt like hell. I could see no alternative except to trust God and give in to his way. I surrendered. To use biblical language, I died to self. In Richard Rohr's book, *Breathing Under Water: Spirituality and the Twelve Steps,* he says, "Surrender will always feel like dying, and yet it is the necessary path to liberation."[8] The "dying" part I felt, not yet the "liberation" part. This whole experience tested my trust in God like nothing else ever has. Rohr emphasizes the decision part of this process: "Our inner blockage to 'turning our will over' is only overcome by a decision. It will not usually happen with a feeling, or a mere idea, or a religious Scripture....It is the will itself, our stubborn and self-defeating willfulness that must be first converted and handed over. It does not surrender easily and usually only when it is demanded of us by partners, parents, children, health, or circumstances." Rohr describes my experience.

What is supposed to happen after one dies to self or surrenders? As Christians, we hope for new life. I know that's what I hoped for.

---

8. Richard Rohr, *Breathing Under Water: Spirituality and the Twelve Steps* (Franciscan Media, 2011), 18.

PART II

Climbing Out

6

———•——

Till Death Do Us Part

The year 1995 quietly rolled into 1996. Jacob and I were getting along better, but I was worried about him. One spring morning I saw him sagged over the newspaper at the breakfast nook, looking pale and gaunt. He had been doing less and less with his business interests and investments. I had been so concerned about him that I was praying a fifty-four-day rosary novena for healing of whatever was wrong with him. He asked me to check his blood. I drew the sample and took it with me to work, dropping it off at the lab before starting my day. Later that morning I was in the exam room with a particularly complicated new patient with two separate malignancies. I heard the knock on the exam room door, excused myself to the patient, and opened the door a crack. My recollections of what happened next are vivid.

The worried-looking technologist from the lab handed me the blood test results. I excused myself and went down the hall to my office, where I closed the door, sat in my chair, and looked down at the results. A shiver ran through me, my body tensed, and I looked up to the heavens. Every result was in the "critical" range. My mind whirled from Jacob slumped over the breakfast table, to his hematologist, to my patient in the room, to the children, and then back to Jacob. What did it mean? Did Jacob have to go to the hospital? Was he going to die? I quickly phoned Jacob and then talked to his doctor, a hematologist/oncologist with whom I worked regularly. An urgent office visit was arranged. I explained to my patient that I had a family emergency. An incredible blessing for me was that this episode occurred during the only brief stretch of my twenty years in practice when I had an associate doctor in my practice. I was able to contact my partner, who took over my patients. I rejoice over the enormity of this grace.

The next few weeks were chaotic. Jacob received urgent transfusions. We researched treatment options for his now aggressive myelodysplasia that was deemed pre-leukemia. We were dismayed to learn that there was no agreed upon "best" treatment. Remember that the internet and email were still quite limited, and we were doing this research by phoning colleagues and experts at major centers and reviewing medical journals. Dr. Edward Weiss, my hematologist friend, brought us a whole stack of relevant journal articles. I am so grateful for my hematology colleagues, both friends and strangers, who guided us through this process with both kindness and professionalism. The hard fact was that some experts recommended bone marrow transplantation, some recommended intensive chemotherapy without transplant, and some recommended supportive treatment only. This last alternative would mean blood transfusions and medicines for comfort only, with no active treatment of the disease. Jacob didn't consider for even one moment this option, no matter how much risk the treatments offered.

At fifty-six years old, he fell into the poor prognostic category of myelodysplasia. We wondered if we should travel to a major cancer center where they had the most experience. Working in radiation oncology for many years had shown me how difficult and risky this type of aggressive chemotherapy can be. Jacob and I soldiered on. We directly phoned the bone marrow transplant experts most known for their expertise and experience. We agonized, trying to make a decision. How could we leave the children for weeks to go to the major cancer center out of state?

I had always observed how much harder it was for my patients to face a serious diagnosis that had no agreed upon best treatment compared to a diagnosis with more agreed upon treatment recommendations. For example, treatment recommendations for colon cancer are usually fairly straightforward with not too many choices. In contrast, men and woman with early prostate or breast cancer not only have to deal with their new diagnosis, but they also have to evaluate and choose from a sometimes bewildering array of treatment options. The same with some more advanced cancers. Making these kinds of choices is very difficult, as Jacob was finding out.

During these three weeks between the blood test and our decision, Jacob also was intensely worried about me and the girls, about our future should he die. He obtained additional insurance and arranged for something called an "accelerated payment" of life insurance, made possible because his doctor certified a twelve-month life expectancy. My journal of his illness describes how he and I were "drawn together by sharing our pain, fear, and tears." Telling the girls was awful.

Context

Let me put all this in the context of our family life. At the time I was handed Jacob's critical lab test results, Serena was in her first year at the University of Florida in Gainesville, located 150 miles north of St. Petersburg. On the surface she seemed to be doing very well, both with her classes and her eating disorder. Sophia was a junior in high school, excelling in everything and enjoying volleyball with a championship school team and later with a competitive traveling private team. Leah was a freshman. She also was doing very well in school and with volleyball, both school and private teams. But she was not entirely happy with the school, which only later I came to fully appreciate. During those years I went to many, many volleyball games, and other sporting events as well—Jacob went to some games too. We wore out a path driving back and forth across town to games and school functions. There were many fun times. The girls were active at school and had plenty of friends, including boyfriends. As I described before, though, the boyfriends had been a source of much conflict and grief in our home.

Since 1989 I had attended Mass every Sunday at my parish. The girls attended the church education program sporadically and reluctantly. Their hearts were not there, but rather at their school with their friends. I had made some close friends in the Bible study I attended for a couple of years after first returning to the church. I had even attended a "Life in the Spirit"[9] seminar led by a bubbly redhead named Michelle. I recently had invited

---

9. Part of Catholic charismatic renewal, these seminars help participants more deeply experience the Holy Spirit.

her to breakfast because I needed a new breakfast buddy, one having moved away and another with a conflicting work schedule. The fact is, however, that we had no relatives and no really close family friends in our area. We had no support system or even neighbors with whom we were close. Before this time we had not completed a Last Will and Testament, except for one handwritten note. Here is another admission that both shames and embarrasses me. The year before, when Jacob's blood test started to look abnormal, he and I had planned to go to Chicago for a consultation about his blood disorder—my only friend in Chicago was a hematologist at the large medical center there where I had worked. For years Jacob had tried to avoid going on an airplane with me unless the children were with us. He worried about them if anything should happen to us. Our plan before going to Chicago (again, I wish I could totally blame him, but I was complicit) was to create a handwritten will in which we would ask my colleague, Dr. Weiss, and his wife to assume guardianship of our children if anything should happen to us. We wrote this will ourselves, signed it, and I think even had it witnessed, before carefully filing it away in our home office. But we never discussed this with Dr. Weiss and his wife. We never asked their permission or informed them in any way. How could we do such an irresponsible thing? The problem was that we never could come to agreement as to who should be guardians for our children. Jacob had limited family in the United States and did not want them to assume the role, and he vetoed my two brothers and their wives. The bottom line was that we had no proper advanced directives.

Decision

Jacob and I endured three weeks of agonizing research, conflicting recommendations, indecision, and confusion. We finally concluded his best option was to go to MD Anderson Cancer Center (MDAH) in Texas for its aggressive chemotherapy protocol. We decided that the bone marrow transplant for his diagnosis was too new, too difficult, and too risky. As we started trying to turn this decision into reality, we found ourselves nervously doubting our decision. On the weekend we finally had made the decision, we awoke on Sunday morning to a long article in Parade magazine about popular scientist Carl Sagan and his diagnosis of myelodysplasia. He had been treated, seemingly successfully, with a bone marrow transplant. Would Jacob do better with a transplant? This incited another flurry of urgent phone calls by us and Jacob's doctor to the transplant doctors mentioned in the article. In the end, we stuck with our original decision.

But how could we just leave town? The girls all were still in their teens. As I described before, we did not have many options. The Holy Spirit whispered in my ear the name of Michelle, the young woman who ran the "Life in the Spirit" seminar. I did not know Michelle well at all, but we recently had gone out to breakfast. I recognized that she was a woman of great faith who happened to be single, without children, and she both lived and worked not too far from where we lived. So I called her, explained our predicament, and asked for her help. The Holy Spirit must have also touched her, because she agreed. We were so grateful. I wrote out a multipage plan for Michelle, the girls, their teachers, and the parents of their friends. That sunny Florida day in March 1996 our three daughters drove us to the airport, Jacob wearing his surgical mask for protection, all of us tearful as we said good-bye. Jacob told the girls he loved them. They gave him cards, written prayers, and a tape cassette they had prepared. It included the beautiful song called *Where There is Faith* by For Him. Jacob and I slowly walked through the door to the plane, solemnly looking back at our girls, then eighteen, fifteen and thirteen years old. It was a wrenching experience.

Bone Marrow Transplant Unit

Although Jacob was not to receive a bone marrow transplant, he was cared for on the bone marrow transplant unit because of the intensity of the treatment and his risk of complications from his experimental multidrug protocol. This was in the day of the protective isolation "bubble room" for bone marrow transplantation patients, where caregivers rarely entered the patient room. Instead, they stood outside the room communicating via a microphone and extending their arms and hands through the sleeves that protruded from the large windows into the patient room that was the "bubble." The families of the patients stayed in a conjoined waiting room that ran along the length of the patient rooms, all with glass windows. We communicated with our loved ones by phones through the window. Sharing and bearing the pain with those other families during those six weeks in the bone marrow transplant unit was one of the most searing and emotional experiences I have ever had. I was there all day, every day. The patients were so sick. The stories were so tragic. Young adults were fighting to live. My husband was fighting to live. I just sat there, trying to encourage Jacob, writing in my journal, reading books such as *Care of the Soul,*[10] and calling home to the girls. Remember that there were no emails or cell phones, so we had to try and connect when we could in the evening. This hospitalization occurred during Lent, the season of preparation for the death and, finally, the rising of Jesus on Easter. I prayed a lot and was able to go to Mass in the hospital. It became very clear to me that death and resurrection were happening on the bone marrow transplant unit—that it was happening with Jacob. The chemotherapy was purposefully strong so that it could kill the abnormal cells in the bone marrow. In the process most all of the normal bone marrow cells also were killed. In the days after the treatment, the blood counts would fall to critically low levels, putting the patients at risk of bleeding and infection. Then, with the passage of days and weeks, the counts would slowly recover. I could see the love and concern of the families, nurses, and doctors. What did this mean? Was Jesus coming to life on this second-floor unit? Was Jacob going to recover in mind, body, and spirit? During Holy Week his blood counts were definitely recovering. On Easter the priest visited Jacob and gave him a blessing.

It was at this time that a poem entered my mind—surprising because I wasn't a poetry person, especially back then. I think my heart was being pierced by the deep sorrow, grief, hope, and love with which I was constantly surrounded during those days, and by all the tears. "Tears are like rain. They loosen up our soil so we can grow in different directions," wrote Virginia Casey.[11]

Here is my poem:

---

10. Thomas Moore, *Care of the Soul* (Harper Collins, 1992).
11. Virginia Casey, https://www.wiseoldsayings.com/tears-quotes/

"My Bone Marrow Has Risen"

Good Friday turns to Easter risen
Death to life, the plan.
Bone marrow cells are put to death,
New life the hope for man.
Platelets die and no more come,
Donors give their love and hope.
In Room 29, the boy fights and dies,
Now there resides a new man's hope.
Jesus falls, the blasts return,[12]
Love and courage grow.
Simon of Cyrene supports him,
Silent, steadfast, just there.
When the killing chemo strikes,
White cells to black depths go.
More love and tears bring strength,
God's Son brings Easter lilies.
"My bone marrow has risen!"
Life to death to life it goes,
Ready should we be.
From fear and pain grow love and faith,
A peace that's meant to be.

Special Graces

It was frightening to enter the bone marrow transplant
unit the first time. Early in my career I had been involved
in the care of some transplant patients and knew how they
often teetered on the painful edge between life and death. I
remember how exhausted Jacob was when we arrived. But

---

12. A blast is an immature blood cell. When too many blasts are found in the circulating blood, it is called leukemia.

when his first nurse walked into the room, his face softened and he visibly relaxed. She was a loving, young woman from Kerala, India, his home. He was greatly comforted by her soft touch, familiar voice, and quiet efficiency.

Soon after we arrived, I was approached by a representative from the blood bank. He explained that, due to the overwhelming demand for blood transfusions, patients and their families were asked to try to supply all the blood products needed by their loved ones. I knew that aggressive chemotherapy killed so many white blood cells, platelets, and red blood cells that transfusions were critical to support the patient in the weeks after the chemotherapy. Patients often needed dozens of units of blood products and could not live without these transfusions. This meant Jacob would need multiple donors to supply the red cells, white cells, and platelets for the blood bank. I took a deep breath, felt tight in my stomach, told the man that I was alone in Houston, and asked, "What am I supposed to do? Where will I get all those blood products?" He gave me a few contacts and suggested I call some churches to get leads. I found out that Houstonians are most generous with their blood donations, for which I was very grateful. One young man told me he always donates platelets twice a week during Lent. Another young woman was active in a volunteer group to visit out-of-town patients and recruit blood donors. Another donor invited me to live at her house while I was in Houston. Yet another invited me for Easter dinner. These kind people and others rallied to our support and supplied donors to replenish the blood bank for Jacob's needs. Thank you, Houston!

Another gift to me was the visit of my twin brother, Danny, for our shared birthday. He visited Jacob, went to

Palm Sunday Mass with me, and took me to dinner at a fancy restaurant. We talked more than we had in years and were greatly moved to find out how similar our life views were. This was the moment when Danny and I really got to know each other as adults and renewed our unique twin bond, a connection that would only strengthen through the years. I'm grateful that something similar gradually happened with my older brother—he had changed so much from the high schooler I remembered. My two brothers are a great blessing for me.

Commingled

It was during those weeks at MDAH that I first started thinking about how the healing of body, mind, and spirit is interconnected. I repeatedly asked aloud at Mass that Jacob be healed in body, mind, and spirit. It seemed that love, peace of mind, and physical healing must be related. I wanted all of that for Jacob. I begged God for that type of healing, if that be his holy will. As I watched young people die in the bone marrow unit, I struggled to understand why some prayers were answered and others were not. Nola's young husband, so sick, was a fervent convert to Christianity. He had been a welder and made beautiful crosses out of railroad spikes. Nola gave one of his crosses to each of us in the waiting area and told us how he had been inspired by the song *Jesus Built a Bridge*, which tells of Jesus using three nails and wood to build a bridge to heaven. But now the welder was dying. Was the prayer insincere, was the love insufficient, was the will to live lacking? How could this much suffering be God's will? I didn't know the answers. I still don't know the answers, but now I can accept this unknowing with more equanimity.

When I recently read what I wrote in my journal during those weeks in Houston, I was reminded of the deep emotions that filled the air we breathed in that space. I described in detail the stories of many patients. Like the two young mothers, one on either side of Jacob, both with relapsed leukemia. One was Anne, whose eight-year-old daughter with a disability had been her donor. Both of these families were from Houston, so the fathers were working to support their families. They always looked exhausted. One time, when Anne's daughter was visiting, I kept hearing the little girl plaintively saying (with the phone, through the window), "Mommy, why don't you talk to me? Why don't you answer me?" Anne had a very sore throat and weak voice on that day and just couldn't make herself heard. Another lovely couple was always there to support Don, their son. He had been diagnosed with leukemia at age 14 and required four cycles of induction therapy to go into remission. Three years later he relapsed and after more chemotherapy achieved remission. He completed high school and then college, summa cum laude. Can you imagine the celebration when he entered Yale medical school that same year? But three weeks after he started medical school, he relapsed. He had to withdraw from school for more chemotherapy and eventually ended up at MDAH for a bone marrow transplant. Unfortunately, he did not do well and died during the time we were there. Ten days after Don died, his father returned to the unit to talk with all of us, thank us for our support, and share the love and sorrow that was overflowing his heart.

During Easter week, I finished reading *Care of the Soul* and commented in my journal how the book emphasized the beauty of shadow, uncertainty, and mystery along with the art and sacredness of life. I wrote, "It doesn't focus thought…it acts like a prism!" I think now I can better understand how those weeks in the waiting room affected me. It wasn't that I learned things. Instead, my soul somehow absorbed the warm commingled blood and tears of all the patients and families. We became one. I was becoming softer, more open on the inside. My spiritual journey to that time had been too much a solo trip, still often planned by me, not God. But at MDAH, as I waited with the others, I experienced the oneness of this community of sufferers. The body of Christ was there. I also experienced how body, mind, and spirit are interwoven into one. With time, I would learn more about how all this relates to divine union and to abundant health.

Next Phase

After five weeks in the hospital, Jacob was discharged, and we returned home to Florida. He required continued chemotherapy and had many office visits, blood tests, and transfusions. Months passed. I returned to work. That summer we managed a couple of beach vacations (one mile from home) for long weekends. The girls helped at home, drove Dad to appointments, and filled in the gaps. My journal of Jacob's illness says the children did all the shopping for Christmas 1996. By that time Jacob's blood was showing leukemic cells. We were advised it was time to start thinking about a bone marrow transplant as a last resort. Could Jacob's family donate bone marrow for him? I can't recall the reason why his one brother in the United States wasn't a candidate. That left his siblings in India. Jacob and I spent the Christmas holidays consumed with trying to get emergency passports and visas for his older

brother and sister, as well as a nephew, to come from India
to donate bone marrow. By February, they arrived, none
ever before having traveled out of Kerala state in southern
India. Jacob hadn't seen his brother and sister for nearly
thirty years. They looked old and frail. His brother, Chettan,
was a match to Jacob so his bone marrow was harvested and
frozen. The stress, pain, worry, and uncertainty for everyone involved was indescribable. The number of leukemic
cells in Jacob's body continued to climb, but other medical
problems cropped up that delayed the actual transplant. By
this time, Jacob was seeing a transplant doctor at Shands
Hospital, part of the University of Florida in Gainesville,
where Serena was attending school. Jacob continued to do
poorly, suffering pain, hoarseness, and cough. For weeks
he had to write notes to communicate because he had no
voice. He was miserable. Jacob finally agreed to a surgical
lung biopsy to find an explanation for the pain and cough.
One difficult treatment he endured was the antifungal
medication called amphotericin B—it is known as "shake
and bake" because of the fever, chills, and violent shakes
that often accompany its administration. We shuttled back
and forth between Gainesville and St. Petersburg. Thank
God I still had my partner who could cover my practice.
Michelle was helping out at home. So many visits, blood
tests, procedures, and doctors. Would Jacob ever be able to
have the transplant? We knew the risk of death from the
transplant was 50%. Without it, 100%.

Sometime later that spring, my partner at work
announced to me that he was leaving. This wasn't a surprise
because there wasn't enough work for two radiation oncolo-
gists at the hospital. He had a more secure opportunity
elsewhere. Even though I sort of expected this change, at

that moment I was jolted by the heavy responsibility of my practice in light of what was going on at home. I had been working most of the year, in between the various hospitalizations, with my partner filling the gaps. So this left me as a solo practitioner at the hospital where I had a contract to provide radiation oncology services. When my partner informed me of his resignation, I told him that I was leaving for the day and went directly to our church. For several hours I sat praying in the pulsing quietness of that sanctuary. Somehow I found some peace with my predicament. As it turns out, the hospital was very understanding, and I was able to make piecemeal arrangements with local colleagues and substitute doctors—*locum tenens*—to take care of my patients and fulfill my responsibility to the hospital.

Girls

This was a very hard year for my daughters. Serena was closest to the stress. Because she went to college in Gainesville, she would often come to the hospital to be with me and her dad. She sat through the "informed consent" presentation for the bone marrow transplant, frightening with its litany of risks. While her dad was still in the hospital and I was staying there in Gainesville with him, she confided that she needed more help with her eating disorder. Somehow we came up with a plan: she would pack up her things (the semester was ending), drive herself home to St. Petersburg, and with the help of her sisters, repack her bags, and then drive by herself to South Florida for three additional weeks of inpatient treatment of her eating disorder. I stayed at the hospital with Jacob. When I read in my journal during my research for this book that she had to drive herself to another city for this inpatient treatment, I was overwhelmed with incomprehension, tears, sorrow, and guilt. How could I have forgotten that?

Leah was finishing her sophomore year in high school, and Sophia was a senior leading up to her graduation. She, like Serena, had been homecoming queen—her dad had not been able to escort her onto the football field, as is the tradition. My twin brother stood in for him. We missed many of the girls' special events. We even missed Sophia's senior awards ceremony when it was announced she would graduate summa cum laude. Her formal graduation ceremony was approaching. Could I even attend?

Their dad's illness didn't mean the girls were supposed to relinquish their friends and activities. Neither Jacob nor I wanted that, at least theoretically. As you already learned, open and trusting conversations were not our forte, even in the best of circumstances, and these were the worst of circumstances. What about the senior trip to Cancun? What about the end-of-year and graduation parties that all the kids looked forward to? High-school drinking and driving was a problem in our community. Some parents resolved the drunken-driving issue by taking the car keys away at the parties and letting the kids spend the night. I remember feeling totally befuddled by all the questions that arose.

Sophia had been accepted by Northwestern University to start in the fall, but we barely spoke of it. She didn't even know if she would be able to attend. By this time, unbeknownst to me, Leah had talked with her sisters about changing high schools, leaving the school where she had been going since first grade.

Because the transplant was delayed to allow for more recovery time from the lung infection, Jacob was discharged from the hospital, and we returned to St. Petersburg. On the day of Sophia's graduation, Adam, our nephew on Jacob's side, came from Atlanta to stay with Jacob at our home during the ceremony—so I was able to attend. Because her dad was so sick, Serena withdrew from the South Florida treatment center to return home early. All three girls were soon home, and all had found summer jobs.

Full Circle

Finally, we had been given a green light for the bone marrow transplant, and Jacob had decided to proceed. The day after Sophia's graduation I packed up and got things organized at home for Jacob and me for our return drive to Gainesville. Adam made us chicken biryani. The gray day wore on. I noted in my journal that the pool was green and that it was drizzling. We were stalling. Finally we said goodbye, but there was no hope or optimism. On the way out, Jacob stopped in our foyer, looked around and said, "I just want to go upstairs and sleep." I ached to tell him to do just that, now, immediately. But I stifled myself, because I knew this was his decision to make. He highly valued his autonomy in making all his health care decisions. Besides, I worried that if I encouraged less therapy, he might think I just wanted him to die. As we drove down our street to leave, I wondered if he would ever see it again. When we reached Gainesville, he was promptly readmitted and given additional chemotherapy as a final preparation for the transplant. But there was to be no transplant for my husband. His condition continued to worsen, and on June 21, his transplant doctor spoke with him, reviewing the alternatives, all which were bleak. Jacob declined further treatment, and, three weeks after we had arrived, we started the drive south on I-75 to return home for hospice care.

Before we leave Shands for the final time in this book, let me tell you about Jacob's transplant physician, Dr. Jan Moreb. From the beginning he and Jacob clicked. He is a soft-spoken and gentle man with Einstein-like curly hair. When he visited Jacob in the hospital, he always brought a gift, his ability to be "present." He acted as if he had not one other thing in the world to do at that moment except be with Jacob. They acknowledged a desire to know each other better and to be able to discuss politics and world affairs. Their special relationship continues to bear fruit to this day as a special friendship between our two families.

The Last Summer

Jacob was very sick. The presence of hospice was a godsend. The caregivers were caring and available. They administered treatments and transfusions that helped Jacob to feel just a little better. He stayed in bed many hours a day. He suffered from pain, nausea, weakness, and, later, waves of anxiety. I made arrangements to be away from my medical practice for as long as would be necessary.

Jacob had been urgently updating his Last Will and Testament and establishing trusts. He completed this process with the attorney. He was intensely worried about me, the girls, and our future. These preparations appeared to give him comfort. He had a spiral notebook in which he wrote notes for me: the bank accounts, locations of circuit breakers and water shutoff valves, location of underground wells, how to take care of the pool pump, and so on. I contacted the funeral home. We had already gone to the cemetery to pick out a "shady" location for his grave. He never liked being in the sun. He also requested a private meeting with Dr. Martin Lewis, a colleague and friend. Martin was a pathologist, but also a minister. Jacob asked him to officiate at his burial.

It seemed like grace visited our home during those weeks. Jacob was more open. He was able to once again say aloud to his daughters that he loved them. These words were always very hard for him to utter. For years it had been sort of a joke, at least for him, to say "ditto" as his response if I told him I loved him. During these weeks with hospice, he accepted his vulnerability and seemed to greatly value the girls and me being nearby. The three girls were all living at home, working their summer jobs, but spending increasing time with him, as well as helping with shopping and meals. He particularly spent time with our eldest, Serena. She told me years later that he spoke to her of his concerns about me, about poor decisions I might make about money and men, how I might let someone take advantage of me. He asked her to watch out for me so I wouldn't do those things. She described to me feeling so confused: happy he was taking her into his confidence and asking for help, yet feeling so conflicted about his requests. Jacob's relatives from out of state came to visit and say good-bye. After his siblings had come from India, there had been more contact with his family. My family called to try to help. My mom was desperate to talk with Jacob one last time to try and repair the relationship before he died. This was not to be. He didn't want to talk with or see any member of my family. Toward the end, the girls and I sat on around-the-clock watch with him. He was becoming more and more lethargic, except for the times when he was jarred awake by coughing, gagging, or panic attacks. The morphine gave him comfort. On August 2, 1997, with his daughters and me hovering over him, he took his last breath. I wrote: "And it was over. So quiet.….His face finally looked peaceful without pain and misery. We held him, kissed him, and cried."

———•———

Our nephew Adam arrived soon thereafter from Atlanta to support the girls and me. Then the funeral home people came to take the body away. I wrote in my journal that they wrapped him from head to toe in "a sheet, tight, like Jesus' shroud. And they took him away. At our request, they uncovered his head from the sheet, and we put on the [University of Florida] gator cap. And, then they loaded him into the minivan."

There was a viewing, a private burial per his wish, and later a memorial Mass. He had stated clearly that he did not want a church service. But thinking of my needs and the needs of my daughters, I made the hard decision (which I often have second-guessed) to proceed with a service at our church and then a gathering for family and friends at our home. We were so honored that Dr. Moreb joined us for the service and gathering. He drove two hours from Gainesville to do so. Jacob would have been so happy—hopefully he would have forgiven me for having the memorial service.

After that, everyone left. The house became quiet and seemed to grow larger. I remember sitting alone in our vaulted living room, transfixed as I studied a bouquet someone had sent to our home. The blooming roses were a pale peach color, and they gracefully arched like a fountain from the simple glass vase. I always remember that bouquet, an indelible, graceful image of love and loss.

Looking Back

First, some advice. Prepare a Last Will and Testament. If you have difficulty choosing a guardian for your children, just imagine someone else having to make that decision for you. The time to talk about death and dying is when you are alive and well. The organization Five Wishes[13] encourages conversation and advanced planning and helps you to get it done. I recommend the book *Being Mortal*[14] by Atul Gawande, as it will open your mind to ways of looking at the end years. Over the years I have repeatedly observed very ill patients undergoing futile treatment, such as weeks of ICU suffering leading to a death that was highly predictable at the time of admission. Sometimes this is unavoidable, but too often it occurs because no honest conversation has taken place between the medical team, the patient, and the family. The painful questions have not been asked: What is the benefit of this treatment? How long will it extend my life? Can it cure me? What are the risks of the treatment? What are the alternatives? What if I decide the risks…the days in the hospital…the operation…the breathing tube… are not worth it to me? Can you keep me comfortable? How can I die at home?

Though I had been an oncologist for years, I never really understood the impact of a major illness on a family until dealing with Jacob's illness and death. Everyone in the family is affected. All routines are disrupted. There is much work to be done. For many there are money problems. There is massive paperwork from doctors and hospitals. There is profound fatigue. There is worry about

---

13. https://fivewishes.org/five-wishes/advance-care-planning
14. Atul Gawande, *Being Mortal* (Henry Holt and Co., 2014).

the unknown. Worst of all, family members must watch their loved one shrink, suffer, and sometimes die. It felt like our family had lived in a bubble full of suffering, a place with a one-way mirror that made us invisible to the rest of the world, which just kept going on as though everything was normal. The lack of nearby relatives or intimate family friends obviously contributed to our difficulties. It is hard for me, even now, to accept how isolated we were during those years. It makes me so appreciative of the special kindnesses I was shown—I still tear up thinking about the chicken soup that Michelle brought, the kindness of Adam, or the understanding shown by my hospital administrator.

In 1997, I was too tired to think about my marriage and what my family had been through. But I would start to notice that life seemed more precious. My children seemed more precious. My family, friends, and community seemed more precious. I rested, trusting that God would be with me as I continued my journey.

7

After the Storm

When I think about the period after Jacob died, I am reminded of the time right after a Florida hurricane. We would gingerly step outside, survey the scene, and usually discover the storm had left a massive tangle of branches, downed trees, soggy ground, and debris blown in from the bay, even unexpected things like someone's entire dock lodged in our backyard. The sun would invariably shine. The air would be fresh. That is how it was after Jacob died. The crisis was over. The sun was shining. But everything was different, and there was much work to be done.

What Is Grief?

First, I had to mentally process what Jacob's death meant. I deeply missed my husband and remembered the good parts of our twenty-seven years together. But I also was conflicted when I recalled the challenges of our relationship. I deeply pondered the meaning of my "Abraham experience," in which I surrendered my girls to God and committed to staying in the marriage. Now, several years after that spiritual crisis, Jacob was gone and the marriage was over.

My grief was complicated. Yes, the marriage brought many good memories, and, best of all, resulted in my having three wonderful daughters. But it was not a happy marriage. I felt profound sadness, and I think I grieved more for the loss of what could have been than I grieved for Jacob. It confused me to consider that he blamed me for our relationship difficulties in the same way that I blamed him. I increasingly recognized my contributions to our unhealthy marriage.

It was disturbing to deal with the uninvited thoughts that snuck up on me, and then wouldn't leave: "I am glad he is dead," "Finally, I am free," or "It feels so good to not have anyone criticize me or yell at me anymore." "I'm so glad I am widowed rather than divorced—I get more sympathy." I even felt a surge of satisfaction bordering on pride, like I had some exalted status, when I heard Mass readings that exhorted caring for widows (James 1:27). I'd study my wedding ring, still on the left ring finger, wondering when and if I should move it. I felt unfaithful to Jacob when I said "my daughters," rather than "our daughters."

Over time I was able to accept that these feelings were honest and valid. It was true that I was free—free to make friends, to move, to change jobs, to mother as I saw fit, to visit my relatives as I chose, and especially to enjoy my days without criticism. I was starting to understand the difference between my thoughts and my feelings—and how vital it was that I give credence to my feelings instead of burying them as I had often done.

Single Parent

Now I really was a single parent. My first priority was getting the girls situated in their schools. Serena returned to college and was able to drive herself north on the same I-95 highway that had carried her father home. One of the things Jacob had done during his illness was take Serena car shopping, initially pushing for a Ford Fusion, but agreeing to a Camry.

Sophia was to start college as a freshman at Northwestern University in Evanston, Illinois. We had to work fast and decided she and I would drive those 1,200 miles together. Planning that trip seemed like a really big deal because Jacob had been the trip planner in our family. Without him, or GPS, I relied on pages of AAA routes and maps. I remember going over the route and arrangements in tedious detail. Sophia and I enjoyed the trip and even stopped in the Hyde Park area of Chicago so I could show her where Dad and I had lived so long ago. It was during this trip that a stark revelation hit me: It was now up to me, and me alone, to remember where I had parked the car or put the keys. There was no one else to do it.

Lastly, Leah transferred from her school of the past ten years to begin her junior year at a different high school, which, fortunately, was near our home. This transition was eased by her joining the varsity volleyball team at the new school. All this happened in the first weeks after Jacob's death.

Then I tackled the mess at home. I sat for hundreds of hours in Jacob's chair in his office sorting through his many files, papers, saved documents, clippings, cards, and memorabilia. To discard anything, even an old greeting card, made me feel disloyal to him—as though he were watching me discard him. We lived in a huge house that I knew I needed to sell. But first I had to catch up on outside maintenance that had been neglected. My calendar was full of appointments with painters, landscapers, arborists, and eventually real estate agents. All this was squeezed into my free time, since I had returned to work six weeks after Jacob's death.

Decisions

I made the first of several big decisions that just seemed to pop into my brain. I would take the three girls to India to visit with Jacob's family. The girls and I had never visited India and, in fact, Jacob had not once returned since we first met. But I felt profound gratitude for his family's help during Jacob's illness. It had been incredibly strenuous and stressful for his much older siblings to make that trip from India. I wanted to help the girls cement their relationships with their father's family. Planning a trip to India seemed overwhelming compared to the trip to Evanston. Remember, we still had no internet or search engines at that time. In fact, Google had just become incorporated that year and was operating out of a garage in California. But I pulled it off with the help of a travel agent. We celebrated Christmas 1998, one-and-a-half years after Jacob's death, in Kerala, India, with our loving and hospitable relatives. The girls and I will never forget our first night sleeping together in a large bed in the home where Jacob had grown up. The ceiling above us was laced with holes—we worried they were worm holes. In the background we could hear the Hindu chanting from the temple next door. A Catholic Church was close by, just down a narrow dirt road surrounded by fields and farms, dotted by occasional trees, cows, and skinny dogs. It seemed we were more than a world away from home. The colorful saris, sumptuous food, teeming streets, tea plantations in the mountains, pepper trees, and beaches of the Malabar Coast remain for me as vivid reminders of a remarkable trip.

I realized on this trip how much better I would have known Jacob had we traveled to India years earlier. I understood for the first time how he understood hospitality: wide-open homes, time freely given, incredible feasts with many dishes for every meal. The second day of our trip we drove from Kayamkulam, Jacob's home town, to Trivandrum to meet more family. Because we were jet-lagged, they offered us a room to nap. Many hours later we awoke to find all the relatives just sitting there waiting for us, the feast also ready and waiting. My daughters and I were shocked to see the subservient role of the women in the family. They never once sat at the table to eat with us—at least not until the last day when we ordered takeout and insisted they sit with us. They spent the meal times hovering around waiting on the men and on us. Then they sat down afterward to eat.

Back in Florida, I listed the house for sale in early 1999. Downsizing to a smaller home was a key part of the plan, so I started sorting through all our stuff and figuring out what to do with the furniture, appliances, books, and so on. It is only when you have to look at each thing you own and decide whether to keep it, discard it, give it away, or sell it, that you realize how much stuff you really have. I recall debating for way too long about a bulky paper cutter that weighed nearly thirty pounds and didn't work very well, but that Jacob had valued. I eventually kept it. The girls had drawers and boxes of accumulated memories with their yearbooks, sports trophies, artwork, letters, and other cherished mementos. This was to be yet another loss for my daughters, as they would no longer have the luxury of keeping everything indefinitely in a large family home. They had lost their father, now they would lose their family home, and unbeknownst to them and to me, they also would be losing their link to their hometown when I moved from Florida several years later. I didn't appreciate the impact of these losses on my daughters.

I bought and moved into a much smaller home, located on a golf course. How strange it seemed to be able to select just what I wanted for that house. I fell in love with a Scandinavian dining room table that featured a slate mosaic surface. I also selected new Mikasa china that matched the green of the kitchen—a step up from the Corelle dinnerware we had used for years.

The biggest decision I made, however, was to leave my medical practice. Just before I left for India, I gave a one-year notice to the hospital. There were multiple reasons for this decision. I considered the future of the treatment facility where I worked to be questionable in light of competition in the city. I wasn't confident my hospital would continue to provide the state-of-the-art radiation treatment equipment that I needed. I felt confined by the narrowness of my specialty. I regretted that I did not know enough about general medicine to volunteer in the free clinic or go on a missionary trip. I yearned to be a "real doctor" and have the freedom to be a volunteer doctor somehow and somewhere. I was blessed because I did not have financial pressures that limited my choices. So I decided that I would leave my practice and learn enough primary care medicine so that I would have this flexibility.

Healing for Our Family

Serena, Sophia, and Leah moved ahead with their lives. They each dealt with all the changes in their own way. I tried to support and encourage them. They did the same for me. Over the years we have talked more and more openly about my marriage and our family conflicts. It hasn't been easy. I've reminded my daughters that I can only describe how it seemed to me and that surely Dad's experience was far different. These conversations were very, very difficult for me. I didn't want to say bad things about their father, especially because he wasn't there to give his side of the story. Furthermore, I still didn't understand my role in the whole mess. With time, they shared more, and I shared more. We shared our pain and confusion. We also laughed at our silly family stories, like when Dad wore child-type arm floats on his own arms when we drove over the new Sunshine Skyway Bridge—he was afraid of heights and couldn't swim. Or how he loved fishing. He would cast the large net off the dock, and then haul in the catch, with the vigorous assistance of Raj, our dog. Who knew that German shepherds liked raw fish? We relived our Sunday afternoon Indian food feasts that sometimes included homemade chapatis made by kneading and rolling out small dough balls. We reminisced about Dad's one specialty in the kitchen, making a delicious Indian crepe called mydexa—it featured coconut and cardamom. We talked about his remedies for upset stomach, which he used his whole life, but especially during his illness. He would put salt and pepper on his tongue. Or, even better, he would put an oily piece of spicy mango pickle on his tongue.

My daughters are all adults now. We acknowledge that Jacob loved us, but the questions remain. Was he depressed?

Did he have a traumatic childhood? Was my marriage to him a tragic mismatch of two wounded people who hadn't sufficiently learned to love, adapt, and grow? Regardless, I painfully concluded that it was through his death that Jacob finally found peace—a peace that appeared to elude him in life. Was this God's plan? What did his death have to do with my "Abraham experience," when I surrendered my marriage and my girls to God? Was Jacob's death necessary for his peace and for the freedom and growth of the four Chacko women? Only God knows the answers.

From this point in the book, I will purposely mention my girls only occasionally. Like most mothers, I love to talk about my children. My life often intersects with theirs and they continue to teach and challenge me. However, I want to preserve their privacy and that of their families. It is enough to say they are wonderful young women living full lives as they move ahead on their journeys.

My Journey

My healing balms proved to be my faith and my friends. After Jacob's death I became more active in my parish and made some wonderful and supportive new friends. I participated in a small Renew[15] group in our parish, meeting regularly for learning and sharing. I also went to a weekend retreat called Cursillo,[16] with its follow-up small-group meetings. These church programs were invigorating for me. The participants, including me, were honest and unguarded as we shared our struggles. These were intimate and deeply fulfilling relationships, some of which persist

---

15. Renew was a program of the Catholic Church designed to help Catholics strengthen their faith; it usually involved small groups gathering in homes.
16. https://www.natl-cursillo.org

even though I no longer live in the area. In the early years after I was widowed, I met and became good friends with other widows. One friendship stands out. I had received a condolence note from Mia after Jacob's death. Mia had lost her doctor-husband the year before. I didn't really know her, but she also was a physician and our children attended the same school. She suggested in the note that, "when you are ready," I could contact her and we could go out to dinner or a show. I waited until several months after Jacob's death and then, using the school phone directory, dialed her number. She answered and, when I said who I was, she just shrieked. There was a pause and then she exclaimed, "What?" She was astounded because at the moment her phone rang with my call, she was holding her phone in one hand and in the other hand the school directory with her finger on my name preparing to call me. Mia and I became dear friends. We not only shared every detail of our husbands' illnesses and deaths as we co-grieved, but we enjoyed many fun outings. The first time we went out to dinner was at a sushi restaurant. I had never been out to dinner with a woman friend (not even once that I could remember), and I had never eaten sushi. It was surreal to sit in that lovely restaurant with not one other thing in the world to do except talk with Mia, drink sake, and enjoy the ritual of eating sushi with chopsticks, wasabi, pickled ginger, and soy sauce. I felt like I was in an alternate universe. I valued my friends and was learning anew how vital they are for well-being and happiness.

Three-Year Plan

I have always liked to plan. Maybe it is more accurate to say that I liked to be in control. The period of time after Jacob's death was a goldmine for a planner. Nothing was holding me back. My daughters were situated, and, as of 1999, were no longer living at home. I wasn't "that" old. I was healthy. I felt like I could do anything. I already described how I wanted to be a "real" doctor and practice general medicine. Somehow I wanted to help the "underserved" pockets of our population. To make that happen, in 1998, I wrote out my three-year plan in a timeline: start learning Spanish, put the house on the market, travel to India with my daughters for Christmas 1998, make arrangements for passing on my medical practice, sell house by late 1999, stop work or reduce hours in early 2000 and "retrain," start new work by end of 2000. While these were all huge decisions, I made them easily and quickly, which reinforced my intentions to more forward. My timeline proved to be remarkably accurate, except for my unrealistic estimate of what it would take to transform myself into a primary care doctor. I really thought all I had to do was study and hang around with my family medicine colleagues for a number of weeks, shadowing them in their offices. But I soon realized how wrong I was.

Haunted

Jacob had been dead for several years. I was really busy, but sometimes I brooded about my marriage. I had started dating a little bit, and this made me think about men and of all my years with Jacob. Whenever I would stop and think about my marriage, I would just gaze up into the sky and silently wonder. A question sometimes popped into my mind, which I would quickly push away because I didn't want to think about it. But the question would continue to intrude and haunt me: "Was I abused?" I don't think I had ever honestly considered this question until then. My constant busyness had helped me to avoid thinking about this chilling word during my marriage and the years immediately following. But the question would not go away...

As I described in the previous chapters, our conflicts started early on. I often acquiesced to his wishes to avoid fights. Sometimes our conflicts were loud, sometimes cold, sometimes silent.

It was a family visit that provoked his first major use of the silent treatment on me. I had taken our first daughter to visit her grandparents. When I returned, he didn't speak to me for weeks. I have a photograph of him holding our young daughter at that time. His face is closed and somber. The silent treatments provoked incredible feelings of helplessness and rage, incongruously paired with attempts to be patient. It was obvious that Jacob wasn't happy. Wondering if he could be depressed only made it harder for me to deal with these feelings. Shouldn't I be patient and understanding if he was sick?

Jacob criticized me often. He didn't like my haircut, he disapproved of my colleagues, and, as I have described, he especially didn't like my mother.

I often thought about that horrible fight when I wanted to take the girls to visit my twin brother and his family in New Mexico. I could still see Jacob blocking the door as we tried to leave for the airport. We were both so angry. I was afraid to force the issue. What would he do if I tried to just grab the girls and make a run for the car? This whole episode was emotionally devastating.

Our daughters' teen years created new issues for Jacob and me—the intensity of our conflicts increased. I know we all suffered. After Jacob's death, when my mind slipped back to these painful, murky places of suffering, I often jerked my thoughts back to the present—I didn't want to remember because it was too creepy. It would take a few years for me to admit that, "Yes, I had been psychologically and emotionally abused." That is what it felt like to me.

Change

In addition to the obvious changes like my marital status and place of residence, I also was noticing internal changes. I had more energy and enthusiasm to live life and concluded this was because I no longer had to bear the heavy burden of daily strife, confusion, and uncertainty. I started to notice another subtle difference, a shift that somehow brought new insights. In ways I don't understand, I think the experience of Jacob's illness and death, including the many weeks sitting with him at MDAH and Florida hospitals, had opened my heart. For example, I was realizing that I needed to heal my pride and sense of entitlement. I had become accustomed to getting privileges and recognition. Doctors were, and I think still are, often held in high esteem and treated with an unmerited deference. I know that I was proud of my MD degree, maybe a little bit too proud. I remember having a personal banker assigned to me when I was in private practice. This happened because I had an MD after my name, a business account, a private account, and a mortgage with this particular bank. The woman banker took me out to lunch and courted my favor. I was delighted with this special attention. I look back warily, hoping I wasn't rude to people. Years ago, in Chicago, our department administrative assistant told me she thought I was arrogant. That wound hurt a very long time—I wasn't able to honestly consider its validity until years later.

I believed that my time was very, very valuable—much too valuable, for example, to have to listen to a detailed explanation by a drug salesman or to wait in a long line at the bank. Somewhere along the way I awakened to the fact that my being late all the time just meant I thought that my time was more important than others'. In other words, I was more important. I had come to value how I was described: "Dr. Chacko, the radiation oncologist with the three beautiful daughters and the big brick house on the water." I started to realize that it would be healthier for me if I were just "Donna," instead of "Dr. Chacko."

My relationship to God was changing. I attended Sunday Mass regularly but did not yet have a committed prayer practice. Talking about my faith and about God was starting to feel less awkward. In fact, I cherished the time I spent with the church groups and was experiencing the healing power of honest, vulnerable faith sharing. Not too long after I moved into my new home in a gated golf-course community, I started getting to know my neighbors. What I did next was pretty bold. I invited all the neighbors to my home for a Mass. My priest friend from Kerala, India, who became our pastor soon after Jacob died, came and, using the slate dining room table as an altar, said Mass for the assembled group of twenty or so mixed believers. I think I offered a meal and recall having good feelings about how the event was received by the guests.

The new dining room table was symbolic of how I was changing. It represented my covenant of hospitality and openness to other people. No more vacant dining rooms for me.

During these years I was very proud of myself for my nightly fifteen-minute weight training workout. But my smugness was disturbed by an intrusive voice in my head: "Donna, why can you find fifteen minutes each evening to exercise, but are too busy to dedicate time for prayer?" I didn't hear God speaking, but I knew he was the source. I listened and started dedicating specific time for prayer.

Looking Back

It is very difficult for me to admit that I felt psychological and emotional abuse in my marriage. I wish there were some other word than abuse because that implies that I was innocent, the helpless victim, and that Jacob was the sole problem in the marriage. That is so misleading.

Early in our relationship, I made choices that effectively handed him the reins to much of my life. Over the years, as I started to grow and change, my clumsy efforts to reclaim those reins were met with resistance. But I did not fully understand what was happening. By then, the patterns were deeply ingrained in our relationship and all we could do was fight, each in our own way. What if I had understood at a younger age what I was doing? Maybe we could have grown and matured together. Or, perhaps, we never would have gotten married at all.

I have never thought of my husband as a bad man. Not at all—I see a man who often was hurting. I so wish for all our sakes I could know and write what Jacob was feeling during these years.

When I look back at the hard times in my marriage, I see myself so muddled that I couldn't think or see clearly enough to understand or take any action. A good childhood, education, and financial security were not enough to prevent this paralysis. I was afraid, unwilling, or unable to make changes or climb out. I accept that I will never have full clarity about my marriage, but I know that I did the best I could, as did my husband.

It was during these first few years after Jacob's death that I really started to understand the value of community. I knew that regular church attendance had been shown in studies to predict better health and well-being. But now I was experiencing this benefit, especially in the small groups, which were beautiful gardens of love, vulnerability, laughter, healing, and God's presence.

My life was changing. Church, prayer, friends, community, and even dancing were bringing balance and connection into my life.

8

Stepping Out

As Y2K approached, I was planning my big retirement party and the details of transitioning from being a radiation oncologist to a family doctor. The latter was more complicated than I had anticipated. To be a competent primary care doctor, I would need to retrain in the specialty of family medicine. This required three years of residency training. When I told my colleagues of my plans, they were absolutely flabbergasted. Stunned. Some thought I was out of my mind to leave what is considered one of the most cushy, high-paying specialties in medicine and enter one of the hardest and lowest paid. Some colleagues expressed curiosity, interest, and encouragement. A few admitted that they wished they too could make a big change, follow a calling, aim higher. They understood and expressed solidarity. For a few months, I was a mini-celebrity in my medical community.

In spring 2000 I was officially accepted into a family practice training program that was based in a large community hospital in my area. Starting July 1, 2000, at age 51, I would be an R1 or first-year resident, previously called an intern.

Humility 101

No longer was I an experienced, competent radiation oncologist. I was an inexperienced intern. During the six months interval between leaving my job at the hospital and starting my residency, I put myself through a crash course in general medicine. I knew that I would immediately be challenged by my limited knowledge of pharmaceuticals. As a radiation oncologist, I only prescribed a handful of medications. But in family medicine, I would need to know everything about hundreds of medications for diabetes, high blood pressure, cholesterol, infections, and so on—indications, alternatives, dose, side effects, contraindications, and drug interactions. I obtained pocket reference books like the *Washington Manual of Medical Therapeutics* and a pharmacopeia. Carrying reference material on my person was vital, since I could not possibly remember everything. I loaded my fanny pack and pockets with: phone, one or two pagers, my PalmPilot (early PDA or personal digital assistant), wallet, keys, pens, ruler, pen light, reflex hammer, stethoscope, books, and a stack of notecards—one per patient. The first Blackberry devices were just coming on the market, so I had no smartphone. My information was a la carte and bulky. With my white coat fully loaded, protruding fanny pack, scrubs, support stockings, and athletic shoes, I was ready. I reviewed the schedule of hospital rotations and clinics. Overnight call[17] varied, usually every third or fourth night. I tried not to think about the possibility

---

17. In 2003, under pressure from OSHA (Occupational Safety and Health Administration), the first major restriction of working hours for medical residents was instituted. Since 2003 was my final year of training and I had less night call by then, I benefited very little from the new restrictions.

of having to work all night long. "Never again," is what I had proclaimed in 1975 when I completed my final night on call during my first internship.

My debut rotation of the residency was in the emergency department. I recall the talkative old woman with a small laceration on her cheek. This was the first suturing I had done in decades. I requested the wrong type of suture and it turned out to be a thread so thin that it was like sewing with a hair. I got very hot and sweaty as I took what seemed like an hour to complete this procedure. A steri-strip is all she probably needed. Then came my first acutely ill patient, an old man with a dangerously fast heartbeat. The attending doctor watched discreetly from his nearby perch, waiting for me to start treatment. He knew that green interns in their first rotation might need a little help. While I was still thinking and planning, he was compelled to come and rescue the patient (and me) with his timely suggestion. In radiation oncology, I had plenty of time to deliberate about how best to plan a course of radiation treatment with the highest chance of killing the cancer and the lowest chance of causing a complication. Leisurely treatment planning was not an option in the emergency department.

Later, during an internal medicine rotation, as I was presenting a patient to the attending doctor at a patient's bedside, the husband of the patient kept peering at me with squinted eyes. Finally he blurted out, "What in the world are you doing here?" I had been his father's doctor years ago for radiation treatment. He didn't understand why I wasn't the attending doctor. I was always having to explain who I was and why, at my age, I was "only" a resident. I may have been older and slower than my co-residents, but I gradually became comfortable in the knowledge that I took very good care of my patients. Each little lesson in humility made the next lesson easier and even humorous.

During these years I studied a lot, easily spending every minute of a day off with my books and journals. I did want to do well on exams, but my motivation to study went well beyond that. I needed information and facts to help me make diagnoses and prescribe treatment. So much was new to me: the rules for interpreting EKGs; recommended antibiotics for sexually transmitted diseases (STDs), pneumonia, strep throat, ear infection, and so on; recommended approach for a fever in a six-month-old vs. a two-year-old; detailed protocols for cardiopulmonary resuscitation (CPR); and, about when and how to treat high blood pressure, elevated cholesterol, or diabetes…and on and on.

Even with all this, I enjoyed myself. I was the matriarch of our class. One time during hospital rounds several of my fellow residents and I were chatting with the attending. Martin, a very smart, young doc with a cute grin, dropped that he had been born in 1974. My mouth gaped, "I graduated from medical school in 1974." Of course, everyone chuckled, including me.

Anxiety

My anxiety grew as I neared my one-month inpatient rotation at the downtown children's hospital. I would be assigned to work with the pediatric residents, including all-night rotations every third or fourth day. This meant all night after working all day. Before this residency, I had not taken care of children, other than my own, for decades. I saw pediatric patients in the residency clinic, but this would be very different—sicker children and more of them. By the time my first day arrived, my anxiety had grown to dread.

Inpatient pediatrics is a high-volume affair, with many admissions and short hospital stays. Every patient needs a full admission exam, orders, history and physical in the chart, daily notes, and eventually a discharge summary with prescriptions. A challenge for me was the dosing of the pediatric medicines—the dose is based on weight, so a mathematical calculation is required. I recall being very stressed by having to quickly do these calculations, particularly with liquid medicines that came in various strengths.

I had to leave home by 4:30 a.m. to get to the children's hospital in time to do "pre-rounds." This meant seeing all the patients assigned to me and reviewing their charts before group rounds began. The hospital did have an early version of an electronic medical record (EMR) system. In fact, it had two totally separate EMR systems: one was for the vital signs, and the second for the labs and other reports. I think the regular patient medical record was still paper. It was during this rotation that I felt particularly old and slow. I was always shuffling my fat stack of index cards, one card per patient, as I struggled to keep track of each patient, the daily lab results, the X-ray reports, and much more. I felt more secure when clutching that stack of cards. There was a certain language and style expected during rounds as the staff and attending saw and discussed all the patients. We had to be efficient with words, have all the relevant information available, and move smoothly with the flow of the team. One time a young attending pronounced in exasperation to the whole group that I did not know how to present a case. What??!!

I was on call my last night in pediatrics. I had worked in our family practice clinic all day and then driven the twenty miles to the children's hospital. I had several admissions that Friday night. I did manage to get a couple of hours sleep in the call room, but felt pretty wrung out on Saturday morning. I struggled to finish all my tasks, so that I could go home. The morning slowly turned into the afternoon. I still had tasks on my list, but felt really lousy. I finally bailed out, surrendered my precious cards to an incoming resident, and dragged myself out of the hospital into the bright warm Florida sun. Partway home I was so sick I had to pull over and vomit multiple times. I recovered from this viral illness… and I recovered from the pediatrics rotation. I "passed" and was ecstatic. One of my co-residents failed and had to repeat the rotation.

We Are One

During these three years of residency, I saw many different kinds of patients, doctors, and diseases and was also fortunate to have amazing travel opportunities. I joined a Jewish group who went to Cuba to learn about its health care system, recognized for its good results and low cost. A life-changing experience was going to Haiti. We offered lessons to children, staffed clinics, and visited the city and countryside. Most memorable was visiting the orphanage. We drove many hours on a bumpy, muddy road, circling up a mountain, to reach the large facility spread under the trees. We saw multiple small buildings and huts with floors of compact dirt, swept perfectly smooth. The children looked happy, walking alone or in clusters, some carrying wood or buckets, many with obvious disabilities. Everything was crude, simple, quiet, and very clean, and this included bandages and rudimentary orthopedic protheses on the many children who had missing or deformed limbs. Some used smooth sticks as walking aids. The images still prick me, reminding me of the great need in our world.

In the United States, I had the revelatory experience of living and working for one month on an Indian reservation in Fort Defiance, Arizona, near the capital of the Navajo Nation. This was the first time I had met a Native American. Seeing the dirt roads and houses dotting the uncultivated expanses of dry land, I got a sense of the lack of hope and opportunity that hung heavy in the dry air. I worked in the pediatric outpatient clinic and was awed by the skill of the pediatricians. A sick baby who needed a rapid evaluation to rule out meningitis would have a full exam, blood work, urine check, and spinal tap done in a flash. Meanwhile, I struggled with the ear exams. It is not easy to quickly and painlessly examine the eardrum of a frightened child, particularly since earwax frequently blocks the view and must be removed. The obesity epidemic had reached Fort Defiance before I got there, as evidenced by the many overweight kids and parents. The hospital was staffed by many National Health Service Corps (NHSC) doctors, a giving and adventuresome group of young men and women. The NHSC offers scholarships to health care professionals in exchange for a commitment to serve in underserved areas.

Seeing so much need in my brothers and sisters was challenging. I bought a small wooden bell in Haiti carved with the words: "No one listens to the cry of the poor or the sound of a wooden bell." I think I was starting to experience what is called moral distress, that is, feeling distress because of a conflict between what your conscience and ethics call you to do and what you are reasonably able to do.

Returning Home

During my second year of residency, my mother's health declined. My oldest daughter was temporarily living with her in Portland, Oregon, and she alerted me to what sounded like early dementia in Mom—clearly more than what we had been calling forgetfulness. I was able to arrange a residency rotation in a Kaiser Permanente clinic near Mom's home, where she continued to live since Dad died eleven years before. Soon, though, I decided to take a leave of absence as Mom's condition was deteriorating. I was determined to do better by her than I had done for my dad at the end of his life. My brothers also were heavily involved, but none of us lived in Portland. We enrolled Mom in an Elder-Care[18] program, which allowed her to have coordinated care and stay home until near the end. My mother had been a strong and independent woman. She had made it clear to my brothers and me that she wanted no artificial feeding or tubes—when her time came, she wanted to be allowed to die. She just gradually stopped eating, lay in her bed a few more days, and then peacefully died. This remarkable woman died at age 90, thankfully unaware of the horrors of 9/11 that happened during her final weeks. She had seen enough and was ready to go.

Seeing my mom suffer and die with dementia was very painful. But my own stress and pain during her illness and decline were far less than the desperate pain and agony I felt during the crisis in my marriage—when I raged at God

---

18. Providence ElderPlace website describes it as "A care model that combines medical care, long-term care, and social services all in one program.

Providence ElderPlace is a PACE program. Enrollees receive complete medical care, medications, medical supplies, adult day care, in-home care, care coordination, transportation and more. All the care and services covered by Medicare and Medicaid."

and my husband and eventually surrendered to God. Nothing in my life, before or since, came close to the anguish I felt at that time. Not my parents' deaths, the illnesses and problems in my family, the weeks of commingled suffering in the M.D. Anderson Hospital waiting room, or even my husband's death. I've long pondered why this is so. I think the answer is that during the crisis in my marriage I was participating in a powerful battle between God, me, and the devil; between my true self and my false self; my will and my conscience; and, paralyzing indecision about what to do. This created an agonizing quagmire of conflict and confusion—like quicksand. It was easier during the illness and death of my husband and my mom, as I had a clear path and just did everything that needed to be done without the anguish of doubt and indecision.

Swinging

During my residency, I was invited by a couple from church to go to a weekly swing dance that included an introductory lesson. This wonderful couple often went out of their way for me, inviting me to their home, family events, and various outings. After first resisting the dance invitation because I wasn't much of a dancer and was too busy, I went and found myself in a classic high-ceilinged ballroom with wooden floors, sparkling chandeliers, and a DJ playing swing jazz music. The regulars stood out with their swirls, twirls, and fancy footwork. To my surprise, I loved it and found the music irresistible. If no one asked me to dance, I asked someone—anyone. I had to move. I still get that urge to move when I hear swing-era songs—like the Andrews Sisters singing "He's the boogie woogie bugle boy of Company B..." No music had affected me like that except the rock and roll of the '60s—except back then I was often shrinking on the sidelines at the dances rather than dancing. The swing music had the magical power to energize me, mesmerize me, and make me want to swing—every week.

This dancing adventure took place about three years after the death of my husband. At first it was disquieting to hold hands with a man other than my husband, to stand close to his body and feel his arm around my waist. But I found I was enjoying the company of these men, who ranged from eager teens to spry seniors. When I realized that I was comfortable to be just who I was with them, I knew I was finally growing up. Now I didn't care if anyone noticed I had brains or held different opinions or wore comfortable shoes. I liked who I was, and I didn't need these men to validate me. Then came my first date in more than thirty years—one of the guys took me to a movie. I admit that I went out with the first man who asked me. He was a nice guy, but I soon realized he was not for me. One of our few dates was a double date with Karen and Lee, the couple from church. To Lee's great glee, I got out of the car with lipstick smears on my face. He still likes to tease me about that evening. One of the several men I dated was about twelve years younger than me and a terrific dancer. This relationship was such a boost for my ego. One time he and I went to Busch Gardens in Tampa—I felt like a teenager strolling around with my boyfriend, and I remember that I even felt pretty. My kissing experiences were initially strange and then pleasing. Mia and I giggled about the details of those first kisses. She hooted, "You did that?" How delightfully fun and silly to chatter about what kind of kiss I had enjoyed. I continued to enjoy my regular swing dances and occasional dates for the next couple of years. It was later that I realized the swing dance experience was my warm-up for what was to come.

Calling

As the three-year residency progressed, I was surprisingly complacent about finding a job. I remember thinking, "Well, God knows I went to a lot of time and trouble to make this change in my career path. I figure he will let me know what to do next." But detailed instructions were not forthcoming. I had a vague idea that I wanted to work in a Christian clinic that offered care for the underserved. I visited a community health center east of Tampa. Specifically, this was one of thousands of Federally Qualified Health Centers (FQHCs) in the United States. Each FQHC is a nonprofit, federally funded clinic that provides comprehensive primary and preventive care, including medical, dental, and mental health, regardless of ability to pay. These clinics are the backbone of the health care safety net in the U.S. During my visit, I saw many Spanish-speaking migrants in the waiting room or waiting for the medicines in the tiny, in-house pharmacy. One-stop shopping and affordable care—I was impressed. But they had no openings for a family practice doctor.

Washington, DC

Toward the end of my second year I still didn't have any plans. Then something happened that made me start thinking about looking for opportunities in Washington, DC. My daughter and I traveled there to go to the high school graduation of my nephew, the son of my twin brother. The ceremony was in the Basilica of the Shrine of the Immaculate Conception, the largest Catholic church in the nation.

Before the service, a man named William overheard me asking for directions to the bookstore and offered to show me the way.

"Oh, thanks," I said, and we set off together. We chatted about DC and books for a few minutes. He recommended *City of God* by Mary of Agreda. They didn't have it in stock, and he quickly said, "What's your address? I'll send it to you." I blithely gave him my contact information, said good-bye, and returned to the church, sliding in the pew next to my daughter. I was more amused than smitten. I leaned over and whispered…."Hey, Leah, this tall, Black dude just hit on me in the bookstore!" Although I definitely was not used to being "hit on," I thought I was coolheaded, even nonchalant. My brother's family would later laughingly describe me as flushed and giddy.

I returned to Florida and continued with my residency. But I recognized that something was different. I walked with a lighter step. I checked the mail every day. A week later a fat envelope arrived from William, the man I had met at the shrine. It was the first of many long letters we eagerly exchanged. Later we added long phone calls. Over the next six months, as I got to know William and his story, I found myself being drawn to him. We came from different worlds. No dating service on earth would have put us together. For starters, he smoked cigarettes, and I abhorred tobacco products. I had completed medical school, and he had not completed college. I was an employed physician, and he was between jobs. I was financially secure. He was not. Our racial difference was the least significant difference between us—I am Caucasian, and he is African American. But I was attracted to his positive attitude, his big laugh, and, particularly, to his deep but simple faith.

I arranged a job interview in Washington for that December of 2002 with the medical director of Unity Health Care, a large group of community health centers. William kindly offered to shuttle me around for my appointments at three separate clinics in the city.

This would be the first time seeing William since our brief face-to-face visit in the shrine six months earlier. We had shared so much of ourselves over the preceding months via letters and phone calls. We were sure we were falling in love. But both of us were cautious. He was recently divorced, having been married twenty-seven years, the same as me before my husband's death. I didn't want to repeat my mistake of jumping too quickly into a relationship.

William was taller than I remembered. It was freezing cold, and he was bundled up and wearing a dark, knit ski cap. We greeted each other with a long, firm body hug and a gentle kiss on the lips. He drove me all around the city to my three appointments, giving me a superb "native Washingtonian" guided tour along the way. It was late afternoon and already dark when he deposited me at the office of the director, Dr. Janelle Goetcheus. She and I chatted about the specific job for which I had applied at Unity.

After I explained what had motivated me to retrain in primary care, she paused and steadily looked at me a few moments.

Then she asked, "Would you be interested in doing something different?"

"Yes," I replied, not having any idea what she was talking about. She reached for the phone and made two calls, to Christ House, a medical recovery facility for the homeless, and Columbia Road Health Services (CRHS), a clinic for low-income families. William had joined us by this time and, before we knew it, the three of us were all headed to Christ House and CRHS Clinic, located nearby in the Adams Morgan neighborhood of northwest Washington, DC.

That cold late Monday afternoon Dr. Goetcheus guided William and me on a tour of CRHS. Then we crossed the street to Christ House. After touring the offices, treatment rooms, patient rooms, chapel, and dining room, we ended up in the community room on the third floor. The room already was set up for the weekly Monday evening potluck dinner for the residential community of doctors and nurses.

I was dumbstruck. I knew this was what I had been looking for, even though I hadn't known what I was looking for. It also seemed so appropriate that William happened to be with me on that tour. Just like me, he could see Jesus at work—in Christ House and in our lives. Something big was happening. God seemed to have answered my prayers about a job. Was he also sending me a joyous God-fearing man to be my partner? I spent the next day with William and then returned to Florida.

During the Christmas holiday that month, William came to Florida for his first visit. My daughters met him and were most gracious, but I know it was not easy for them. Loose and relaxed, William was very different from their father, a dignified man who had been most comfortable in neckties.

I continued my residency. I prayed more. I giggled about William with my female friends. During my trip to Haiti, he managed to send me a letter that arrived while I was there with the group of volunteers. The women and I all giggled as I read parts of his letter to them. I swung back and forth. One moment I felt totally tranquil with everything going on in my life. The next minute I felt like a lovestruck teenager whirling in circles.

That spring I made a two-week visit to Washington and spent some time working in the clinic and at Christ House. Everything was becoming clear. I made the firm decision to leave Florida and relocate to Washington, DC, to work in the clinic and Christ House. After all, God had plans for me there. He had arranged a job, a residential community, an apartment, a ministry, a man, and even a parking space. I couldn't say no.

The Move

In June 2003, I completed my residency. With my daughters all home from college, we threw a huge party to say goodbye to our many friends and colleagues in Florida. William came from Washington, DC, to join the celebration, as did my two brothers, Danny and Dave. A great joy of these years was the increased contact with my brothers, Danny, the doctor, and Dave, the lawyer—honest, hardworking, family men who, like me, have learned from their ups and downs in life. I knew they would do anything for me, and I think they knew the same about me.

My planned move to Washington required further winnowing of my possessions and our household goods. I understand now that I didn't recognize how hard this was for my girls. They were losing their Florida roots. Their Florida home base. Their hometown storage facility. Their permanent link to the only place they called home. To ease the space crunch, I rented a storage facility in Gainesville, where my youngest daughter, Leah, now lived. Jacob's doctor, Dr. Moreb, and his family in Gainesville were persuaded to take our baby grand piano on "indefinite loan."

This family also later ended up adopting Serena's two dogs when she moved to Oregon. Through the years, both Serena and Leah would live with the Morebs for short periods, and years later, Leah, along with her husband and two children would temporarily live in their home. This family friendship proved to be an unexpected positive by-product of a very painful time for our family.

Finally all the boxes were packed. Serena would accompany me on the drive to Washington. After watching the moving van pull away, we unceremoniously drove off in my very full Honda Accord. I was surprised how easy it was to leave Florida. The miles flew by and soon we were driving through Virginia. I stared at the signs high above each of the four northbound lanes of I-95 announcing "Washington, DC- Washington, DC- Washington, DC- Washington, DC" So many signs pointed to Washington!

Looking Back

I entered medical school in 1970 when Nixon was president, stamps cost six cents, and a Boeing 747 revolutionized travel by making its first commercial passenger trip from New York to London. Health care also looked very different from my vantage in a twenty-first century residency training program. Dramatic advances had taken place in pharmaceuticals, laboratory testing, imaging, and surgical techniques. Medical education also had changed. I had originally been taught in a disease-based system. I was taught to evaluate a patient, diagnose the disease, and then administer the proper treatment. In 1970 mind-body medicine was in its infancy in the United States, so the influence of the mind on disease and health was underemphasized. Unhealthy habits received scant attention. During medical school, we had minimal instruction about nutrition. The health risks of smoking had only been presented to the public six years before I started medical school, in the landmark 1964 Surgeon General's report. Not everyone, including doctors, accepted the findings—after all, 40% of Americans smoked, including health care professionals. It was only when I practiced radiation oncology that the tragic toll from smoking became clear to me. Probably forty percent of my patients had smoking related cancers that too often were fatal—particularly advanced lung cancer.

Looking at the whole picture, the progress has been undeniable. Life expectancy improved every year, from 70.78 years in 1970 to a peak of 78.93 in 2010.[19] Unfortunately, the health of our nation has stopped improving. Even before the COVID-19 pandemic, in 2017 there was a dip in life expectancy in the United States. We face rising chronic disease rates, obesity, depression, suicide, gun violence, and opioid addiction. The reasons for these modern challenges are complex.

One explanation is the tendency of the profit-based U.S. health care system to prioritize use of medicines, testing, procedures, and operations over primary care and self-care. In family medicine, we were taught to encourage self-care, counseling, and healthy habits, instead of always jumping to medications, injections, CT scans, and specialty referrals. In my experience, patients (and some doctors) underestimate the risks from medicines or treatments and overestimate the potential benefit—this attitude contributes to complications and poor outcomes. Other factors are the lack of access to health care, income inequality, and injustices that persist in our society.

19. https://www.macrotrends.net/countries/USA/united-states/life-expectancy

Suffering is so much more than a list of diseases. I know how much my family suffered because of the marital strife between Jacob and me. I saw in the family medicine clinic how stress from relationships and difficult life circumstances aggravated pain, blood pressure, and diabetes. I was starting to appreciate how suffering of the mind, body, and spirit could become so tangled as to create a hard knot that was very difficult to unravel.

As a doctor I had begun to think much more broadly about the path to abundant health. I was excited about moving to Washington, DC, but didn't know how much more I had to learn.

9

The Other Side

My new home in Washington, DC, was a sunny, two-bedroom apartment in Kairos, the four-story apartment building owned by Christ House. Residents included staff in three apartments and about forty "graduates" of the Christ House program in the remainder. The latter were all previously homeless men, mainly African American, and most in recovery from addiction, mental illness, or a slew of health problems. They also were the most grateful and welcoming bunch of folks I had ever met.

You can't miss the nearby Christ House on Columbia Road, N.W. Just look for the statue of Jesus bent over washing the feet of a pauper and for the cluster of residents lounging around in front of the building. In the late '70s Dr. Janelle Goetcheus was a family medicine doctor working in a small clinic near where Christ House is now located. One cold winter day in 1983 she tried in vain to help a homeless patient find services and housing. The next morning this man was found frozen and dead in a nearby phone booth. His death propelled Janelle into action to prevent this from ever happening again. An anonymous person donated $2.5

million. Janelle and her co-founder husband, Rev. Allen Goetcheus, purchased a four-story building and founded Christ House, a nonprofit that opened its doors in 1985. Janelle and Allen and a loyal, hardworking staff continue to this day helping the most vulnerable of the homeless in our nation's capital, those too sick to survive on the streets, but not sick enough to be hospitalized. As of 2019, Christ House has counted more than 9,000 admissions of homeless individuals. In 2019,[20] Christ House provided health care for 249 patient admissions and 9,228 patient-days of care. There were 150 participants in the nine-week New Day addictions recovery program. And 67% of patients were discharged to more stable housing than before coming to Christ House. Christ House was one of many life-giving ministries that sprung up in the area, all seeded by the inspiration of Rev. Gordon Cosby and the Church of the Saviour[21] community. This was "church" in the fullest sense.

In addition to working at Christ House, I also worked at Columbia Road Health Services (CRHS), the small out-patient clinic located kitty-corner from Christ House. I joined six doctors and two nurse practitioners, our mission being to serve the needy with love and respect, regardless of ability to pay.

Settling In

First things first. Getting to know William and his city was my priority. Except for short visits, he and I hadn't spent much time together since we met a little more than

20. Christ House 2019 Annual Report

21. Learn the history of the most remarkable Church of the Saviour at https://inward-outward.org/about-us/ and https://www.pbs.org/wnet/religionandethics/1997/10/31/october-31-1997-gordon-cosby-and-washingtons-church-of-the-savior/15297/

a year ago. He lived two miles north of my apartment and traveled by bus for his new job and to visit me. William introduced me to his city, of which he knew every inch. We talked on the phone every day and saw each other several times a week.

Going on long walks down Columbia Road to Dupont Circle, or up to Connecticut Avenue, the National Zoo, the National Cathedral, or as far as Georgetown and JFK's old home didn't seem real at first. I was thrilled each time we walked by famous places like the White House, Ford's Theater, National Geographic, Kennedy Center, or the Watergate Hotel. Even walking on errands and being able to stop at the grocery story, the pharmacy, and the post office all in one trip was exciting. I hadn't ever seen neighborhoods with row houses and folks sitting on their stoops except on Sesame Street. It was a novel experience to go for a walk and see colleagues, friends, and patients along the way.

William and I quickly fell in step. Saturday we would go grocery shopping together, including the supermarket, the produce store, and sometimes the Florida Market, where William had been going for years to get his "meats." I'd never seen anything like it except on TV: a sprawling warehouse-like place with a sawdust-covered floor, crowded with mainly African Americans, and overflowing stands of fruit, cheese, veggies, CDs, clothing, perfumes, and meats—things I didn't recognize stacked or hanging from the ceiling. William was right at home, but at first I was cowed and stayed very close to him. This was the first of many experiences when I would be one white face among many Black faces. Sometimes William had the opposite experience when he accompanied me to certain events, like several years later at one particularly memorable wedding of a family friend in Miami Beach, when he was the only Black, other than the servers, among the 500 in attendance.

Christ House Stories

At Christ House, I was in charge of the residents assigned to my team—to admit them and see them at least weekly, while working closely with the nurse practitioner who worked full-time in the medical unit. Our weekly interdisciplinary team meetings included me, the nurse practitioner, case manager (social service), addiction counselor, and the spiritual counselor. Here we would discuss each patient's progress, determine what treatments were needed, and start the slow process of making a long-term plan. Always challenging was finding housing or placement. Sometimes all progress halted for weeks or months until a birth certificate could be obtained. Same story for obtaining benefits or getting appointments. I would care for these men during their stay in Christ House, which ranged from one day to more than one year, and sometimes continue as their doctor if they did well and were able to move into Kairos House, where I lived.

James was lean, spoke with a perpetual monotone, and laughed freely. Born in 1946, for years he worked as a distributor and lived in the neighborhood. After thirty-five years of alcoholism, he finally lost everything and became homeless. Then he broke his leg in a fall, had leg surgery, and, at hospital discharge, was admitted to Christ House. He remembers that two weeks before his accident he had begged God for help—his life was not worth living. At Christ House, he followed medical advice and participated in AA meetings, church, the addiction program, and individual counseling. He admitted having stayed angry with God after the death of his mother, until he finally "got back with God." Now, many years later, he has a job, works as a volunteer, has started writing and singing songs, and, most joyfully, is very involved with his extended family.

Getting to know Williard, another patient, changed forever how I looked at street drunks. Years before I arrived, he had been admitted nineteen separate times at Christ House and each time quickly returned to the street and his bottle. The last admission worked. When I met Williard, he was an older, highly respected Kairos resident, AA leader, and dining room volunteer who already had been in recovery for ten or fifteen years.

Wallie was a near-silent man who legally emigrated from Thailand to settle in Canada. Seeking warmer weather, he came south and ended up living on the streets in Washington, DC—vulnerable because of his mild autism and diabetes. His feet froze and, after a partial amputation of both feet, he came to Christ House. With daily wound care his feet finally healed, but he would remain nonambulatory. So, with no papers, no ID, no money, and wheelchair-bound, we knew placement would be very difficult. It would have been impossible if not for Gift of Peace House, a nursing home facility opened by Saint Teresa's Missionaries of Charity in 1986. Wallie moved there and came to CRHS for his follow-up visits with me. He was able to obtain his diabetic medications because Washington offered limited health benefits to undocumented citizens. Wallie's weight and blood sugars slowly increased, and I kept increasing the dose of his oral medications and counseling him about his eating. If Wallie would ever reach the point of requiring insulin to control his diabetes, he would have to leave Gift of Peace—they were unable to offer care for any patients who needed injections.

I can still see the new admissions who came directly to Christ House from the streets. They were often African American, hunched over and sullen, looking broken and defeated. Their clothes were stiff and black, starched by embedded dirt, sweat, and sometimes urine. The black, plastic garbage bags they clutched contained their every possession. After the staff member slowly explained the procedures, he or she would gently escort the new resident for his first shower. The aid would assist as much as necessary, helping to peel off the smelly clothes. Caution was needed to remove socks, as the skin often would be ulcerated or scabbed and easily pulled off along with the socks. Lice and scabies were not uncommon.

Every patient was different, but there was an oft-repeated miraculous transformation that I witnessed in many of them. Starting with that first shower and first night with a soft bed and clean sheets, they started healing. The primary remedy was the unwavering love, respect, and compassion showed to them by the staff. The men slowly started sitting up, looking around, and opening up. I'm not saying it was easy or uniform. We saw: withdrawal symptoms; untreated mental illness; accumulated wounds from lives that had begun with neglect and abuse and ended up with years in jail or on the street; and the pull of addictions that took residents right back out to the streets. They were always free to leave, like Cliff did. William, who had a temporary job driving the Christ House van for a couple of years during the period he was back in school, told me Cliff's story. This older man's need to get high was too much for him. He insisted on leaving Christ House. One rainy day, William was asked to take Cliff wherever he wanted to go, which ended up being a deserted street in a poor section of southeast Washington, evidently his "hood." William left him and drove away, seeing him standing alone in the near-dark, clutching his plastic bag of belongings.

During my time at Christ House we had several patients who had been paralyzed by gunshots. Each was a strong, handsome, young, Black man; and each was wheelchair bound forever, equipped not with a gun but with a urinary catheter. For months, our team struggled with placement for Jack, one such resident. His home was a basement apartment at his uncle's house—and it had no wheelchair access. What were the alternatives? Which group homes or nursing homes would take him? Did they have wheelchair access? Many of these gunshot victims, like so many of our patients, urgently needed drug rehab programs, further complicating the placement process.

I had never seen a patient dying of AIDS before coming to Christ House. HIV-AIDS treatment wasn't as easy, accessible, or successful as it is now. Dr. David Hilfiker,[22] one of the original Christ House doctors, had opened a hospice home for AIDS patients, later for cancer patients as well. I remember visiting some of my patients at that welcoming haven for the dying. With its soft drapes, cozy furniture, and folks playing cards in the living room, it certainly didn't look like a home for the dying. After a death, the entire family of Joseph House grieved together with a tender, prayerful service. In spite of huge public health efforts and some progress, HIV continues to plague our nation's capital. In 2019, 12,322 DC residents or 1.8% of the population lived with HIV.[23]

---

22. Learn more about Dr. Hilfiker in his book, *Not All of Us Are Saints: A Doctor's Journey*, (Ballantine Books, 1994).
23. https://dccfar.gwu.edu/dc-department-health-releases-2019-annual-hivaids-epidemiology-and-surveillance-report-washington-dc

A number of HIV-positive Kairos men have virus counts that are low or "undetectable," as was the case with Henry. He told me his problems began when he first used marijuana, then continued with methamphetamines, and finally crack, which controlled his life for thirty years. He was getting sicker with weight loss, fever, accidents, and depression. During all this, Henry continued to work, earned $150 on a day job, and spent it each night on drugs. He left after a brief stay at Christ House, but he resisted coming back until one night in desperation Henry returned to Christ House with his many problems—history of abuse as a child, addiction, homelessness, suicide attempt, HIV, cancer, hepatitis C, and kidney failure. When I got to know him as my neighbor, he had a staff job at Christ House, was an active volunteer, and a man loved by all.

My work at Christ House was my first up-close experience with addiction and with the twelve-step program, the foundation of Alcoholics Anonymous. I saw how its emphasis on surrender, community, honesty, and a higher power can be a healing balm for all of us. AA meetings were held regularly, and a formal nine-week addiction-recovery program called New Day was offered. Kairos was full of New Day graduates who were joyful and free. One of them was Will, a friendly and outgoing guy. He was an alcoholic in recovery, doing well with his hepatitis C and liver cirrhosis. One bright, spring Saturday morning he and I decided to go to the jail to visit another Kairos guy who had been arrested on a probation violation. We took three different buses to get to the DC jail. The waiting area was a dark place crowded with family members, including many children, waiting to visit their loved ones. We found Walt to be quiet, but doing OK in the jail—he was released a few weeks later. I greatly valued that all-day trip with Will, but unfortunately he didn't do well. He was one of the small minority of New Day graduates who relapsed. He started drinking and soon was back on the street. Alcohol is a liver toxin, injurious to all and perilous for Will with his liver disease. I don't know how his story ended. I'm guessing that 30-40% of my Christ House patients had hepatitis C as a result of their drug use—they did fine as long as they stayed off alcohol.

Christ House Church

A loyal community of current and past residents of Christ House and Kairos, staff, volunteers, supporters, friends, and neighbors attends the Sunday worship service in the dining room of Christ House, which was converted to a church every Sunday. William and I became part of this community.

Gratitude, social justice, and the challenge to listen to and follow God's call were proclaimed in powerful ways, as we sat there surrounded by men and women recovering from unimaginable brokenness. The small gospel choir filled the air. In my early years at Christ House, the choir had a Black and blind pianist who pounded the keys, swayed, and sang like Stevie Wonder.

Since William and I were Catholics, we also attended the 7:30 a.m. Sunday Mass at Blessed Sacrament Catholic Church, in Chevy Chase Circle, near where William lived and where he attended weekday Mass. Blessed Sacrament is a large, affluent parish that was very welcoming to us. Both the Catholic Mass and the Christ House service used the identical scripture readings, had heartfelt homilies, offered Communion, and were prayerful gatherings of sincere people trying to serve God. I sometimes pondered

the huge contrasts between these two groups of worship-
pers—in terms of race, health, income, opportunity, safety
network, and so on.

Columbia Road Health Services

Four days a week and some Saturday mornings I saw
patients at Columbia Road Health Services. The clinic was
a very cozy, two-level structure with ten exam rooms; the
two floors were connected by a steep, narrow staircase that
climbed from the waiting room. Most of the staff spoke
English and Spanish, and some spoke Amharic, which was
fortunate for our Ethiopian patients. Medical assistants
served as translators. The first year I arrived in Washington I started studying Spanish, but for a long time I had
to rely on the translators (or our phone dial-up translation
service for other languages). By the time I retired I often
saw Spanish-speaking patients on my own, but my limited
Spanish was always a challenge for me and these patients. In
addition to immigrants from Central and South America,
we also saw African immigrants, African Americans, and
Caucasians. These diverse patients helped me understand
the struggles that many immigrants face.

Yesenia was a young woman recently immigrated from
Central America. She spoke no English, had no job, and lived
in the corner of her aunt's house near the clinic. The rest of
her family was all in Central America, and she was desperate to send money to them. But she was jobless, lonely, and
didn't feel well. Over and over she came to the clinic with
depression, insomnia, and headaches. I cared for her and also
referred her to social service and the clinic's mental health
counselor. Then she didn't appear for six months. When she
returned, she looked like a different person. She was smiling,

bright, and had no health complaints. She proudly told us of starting English classes at the nearby DC public charter school devoted to English-as-a-Second Language. She had made friends, was speaking a little English, had a part-time job, and only came to the clinic for a Pap smear.

Leo immigrated to the United States and immediately had a brain seizure, caused by a parasite infection in the brain. He required emergency brain surgery and medicines and afterward was told he was fine and that he needed no more treatment. Leo arrived in our city soon thereafter, still frightened about his diagnosis. He had headaches and was convinced the parasites had returned. Feeling very anxious, Leo repeatedly sought help in our clinic and in multiple emergency departments in our city. I cannot count the number of normal brain CT scans he had, usually ordered in the emergency room by a doctor who did not know him. All this aggravated Leo's insecurity, worry and, alas, his headaches. He returned again and again to the clinic for help and answers—he would relax and feel better for a short while. No parasites were ever found, but this cycle continued for nearly two years, until Leo got himself situated with a job and friends. The headaches resolved, and his anxiety greatly improved.

Sylvia was a sweet woman who had diabetes, severe high blood pressure, and a fifteen-year history of a very slowly growing malignancy. Her adult children drained her emotionally and financially to the degree that she felt abandoned and alone, even though her son sometimes lived with her. Her grief and anger over her family and financial situation were dominant and wreaked havoc on her blood pressure. Each visit was awash with tears and exclamations of sadness and grief. Her blood pressure and diabetes were out of control. She had gradually stopped thinking about God—all she could think about were her stresses and problems, the latest being her likely eviction. Even with referrals to psychiatry, counseling, and social services, she was unable to move in a positive direction during the years I was her doctor.

A recurring question for me was why these patients had multiple illnesses—not just two or three, but eight or ten. Doctors expect illnesses to sometimes come in clumps. The classic example is obesity, diabetes, high blood pressure, and heart disease all afflicting the same patient. I didn't expect to also see liver disease, autoimmune disease, cancer, colitis, and various pain syndromes. At that time, I blamed these problems on stress and unhealthy habits. Maria cleaned hotel rooms during the night. Then she babysat her grandbaby during the day. She sent money home to El Salvador. Her husband drank too much. Concentrating on stress reduction, healthy eating, and exercise were not on her agenda. Her body ached, especially her shoulders. Her blood pressure and weight were going up. Her liver tests were abnormal, and eventually she was found to have fatty liver disease. I learned about this condition during my family medicine residency, but didn't expect it to be so common. Maria was not alone—we saw this condition every single day. One lovely woman named Teresa also was under stress and was only a little bit overweight. After monitoring her carefully for a few years, I was shocked to diagnose liver cirrhosis—on top of her diabetes, high cholesterol, and migraines. The fatty deposits in Teresa's liver had caused inflammation and created a condition called nonalcoholic steatohepatitis or NASH. This can lead to scarring in the liver, the hallmark of cirrhosis. In the US, hepatitis C, alcoholic liver disease, and NASH are the three leading causes of liver cirrhosis that leads to liver transplantation.

I also was surprised by the frequency and variety of pain complaints. Overwork injuries were common, like the shoulder pain I described in Maria. When I asked a patient, "Where do you hurt?" I often heard, "todo el cuerpo." It hurt everywhere.

One woman came to me dozens of times over several years for right-side upper abdominal pain, just below the ribs. Her pain was real and severe, but seeing her was very difficult for two reasons. One, despite all the lab tests, CT scans, ultrasounds, and referrals to specialists, there was no diagnosis. Two, she was histrionic during the visits, talking loud and fast, not stopping even to breathe. She finally got some relief from seeing our in-house therapist, whom we were so blessed to have. Diane was a licensed clinical social worker, fluent in Spanish, and had been immersed in Latin culture for years. Countless times she was able to help a desperate patient, often uncovering sordid details of abuse, neglect, and hopelessness. This patient's care was ongoing when I left the clinic.

Not all of our patients were immigrants. Across the street from the clinic was a large apartment building where Jane lived. She was a highly intelligent, single woman with serious mental illness and agoraphobia. She relied on her case manager from one of our many fine and overworked mental health agencies. When she finally could get to the clinic, she would bring an organized list of questions. Her psychiatric medicines led to continual weight gain and diabetes, common side effects. But she was so brave and just kept plugging ahead in spite of all her health and money problems.

One of the world's 154 L'Arche[24] residential communities is located in Washington, DC, near the clinic. This special place is home to those with intellectual disabilities and to the resident volunteers and staff who assist in their care. I had dinner once at their home and often saw residents strolling in the neighborhood. They always appeared to be very happy. I loved L'Arche, but have to admit that seeing the residents with intellectual disabilities in the clinic was a challenge—especially for their yearly physicals. Federal and Washington, DC, laws protecting the disabled required detailed documentation of health and care. I was required to prepare a thick packet of notes, test results, and completed forms. I did all this type of paperwork after seeing the last patient of the day— there was just no time in a fifteen-minute visit.

Joey was one of my pediatric patients. I first met his teen mom when she came to the clinic late in an evening shift, soon after I started working there. She had severe shortness of breath from uncontrolled asthma. This second-generation young mom lived with her son and her Nicaraguan mother in a one-room studio that always had the TV on. Joey missed his routine wellness visits, his immunizations were behind, and he wasn't reaching his developmental milestones. I was saddened to see him drinking a baby bottle full of pink milk at some visit when he was two-and-a-half or three years old. Referrals were made for developmental testing and social service help for Joey and his mom. He continued to be behind benchmarks and spoke only a few words.

Then I heard his mom got pregnant again and had an abortion. She made these arrangements herself—I didn't

24. https://larche-gwdc.org

refer patients for abortions, nor did anyone in our clinic, as far as I know. I accept the teachings of my church that abortion is wrong. But I have to admit that the eyes of my heart see abortion more as tragedy and failure than evil or sin. Wasn't Joey's mom's abortion at least partially the result of failures of health care, education, family, church, or a society that often encourages sex as pure recreation—love and commitment optional? Had I and others failed to provide enough support to this challenged teenager? Had we failed to offer resources so she knew she wouldn't be alone with her baby? Had we failed to encourage her to practice abstinence or reliable contraception? I'm deeply challenged by these questions, and all I can say is that I'm glad that our merciful God is the ultimate judge.

Even though my religion disapproves of artificial birth control, my conscience is clean about prescribing contraception to patients who had no interest in abstinence. But the actions of one of our other doctors in my clinic did make me stop and think more deeply about the question of contraception.

My colleague, Marie, also a Catholic and a very good friend, decided her conscience would no longer allow her to prescribe artificial contraception. After she announced this to her patients, they would sometimes come to me or other doctors to get their pills or IUDs. I agree with Marie that it is a joy to see a couple so committed to each other and to God that they joyfully practice abstinence or natural family planning to best honor God and their bodies. But from what I saw in the clinic, it is a rare couple where both the man and the woman are motivated enough to make it work. I always think about Joey and his mom—and the many others like them. I deeply reflected on this question, prayed about it, asked God to guide me, and ultimately decided I was doing the right thing by offering all kinds of contraception to my patients.

Seeing so much need and stress in peoples' lives was challenging. Dealing with late patients, missed appointments, obstacles to care, changed formularies, updated record systems, and volumes of paperwork also was difficult. When I witnessed that other providers with similar challenges appeared to be less stressed than me, I felt inadequate. Was I not organized, smart, efficient, or as generous with my time as they? What about my mission to serve those in need? I needed to be patient and gracious, not irritable. Sometimes I resented giving too much of my time. Or, I chastised myself for not making that one more phone call to try and reach the gastroenterologist about my liver patient, talking again to the therapist about my new patient's serious depression, or bugging the insurance company about treatment they denied.

Not being able to consistently meet the needs of my patients was stressful and sometimes profoundly disturbing. But I pushed forward, not knowing I was setting up the kindling that would one day flare into raging burnout.

There was one part of my life that was stress-free. The William part. After we spent several years getting to know each other better, I knew for sure he was for me—I really loved and respected this man. Thankfully, the feeling was mutual. We were married in 2006 at our parish, Blessed Sacrament Catholic Church in Washington, DC. He moved into Kairos with me, and we enjoyed our surprisingly easy relationship. William is a fun, affable, hardworking man of God, and I was very grateful he was my husband. He graduated college with a business degree and started his new career. But having William in my life wasn't enough to stop my gradual burnout. Here's how it happened.

For the Record

I was one of many doctors who struggled to efficiently use computerized record keeping or electronic medical records (EMR). To have more time with my patients, I tried various strategies: writing shorter notes; reviewing the patient's case ahead of the visit; completing the notes after the visit or at home; or using templates. In 2009, my sixth year in Washington, I started to drag and feel more stress. I was frequently behind schedule, frustrated by my still inadequate Spanish and the demands of record keeping. But I was coping—until we got a new EMR in 2010 when our clinic officially merged with the much larger Unity Health Care. This consolidation required Columbia Road Health Services (CRHS) to merge its EMR with Unity's system.

Implementing EMR fully into the U.S. health care system was a priority during these years. In 2009 the federal government set aside $27 billion for an incentive program[25] to encourage full adoption of electronic health records systems, or EMR. To achieve "meaningful use," doctors and clinics were financially incentivized to rapidly expand their EMRs to include data collection, patient education, and portals for patients to access their medical information and their doctors.

We were reassured all steps would be taken for a smooth transition to the new system, including training, data

---

25. Medicare offered dollar incentives to clinics to encourage use of EMR starting in 2011 and ratcheted up each year after that. https://www.cdc.gov/ehrmeaningfuluse/timeline.html

transfer, and reduced schedules during the conversion. I don't question anyone's intentions. But for me, this process turned out to be a slow burn that first stung, then blistered, and eventually became full-blown burnout.

Unfortunately, in the merger of the two systems, very little of each patient's record automatically transferred from our existing EMR to the new system. This meant that the patient information either had to be copied from the old and then scanned into the new system or manually entered by the doctors. I found myself spending many hours ahead of each session filling in the patient record with the information I needed. When was the last Pap? What about immunizations? When was the new blood pressure medicine started?

The expanding "meaningful use" requirements for the EMR resulted in a continual series of upgrades to the system and an ever-increasing number of "clicks" for the doctor, as we entered the data required by our clinics in order to meet the guidelines. Sometimes this increased data entry improved care, but often it did not. If we clicked that we had informed the patient about anything (the risk of immunizations or medications, the need for a low-carb diet, the risk of smoking, and so on) and then clicked the print button for a multipage patient information handout, the patient education requirements were officially met. But the patient frequently learned very little—he/she rarely read or digested all that information and the amount of face-to-face instruction too often was insufficient.

With the implementation of the new EMR, our clinic also adopted a new billing system. It now became the job of the doctors and nurse practitioners to enter into the record the detailed billing codes for each service at every visit. I had long accepted the requirement that we understand the complex diagnostic codes. But also being responsible for the billing codes was hard to swallow. In addition to billing, the data also was used to accumulate productivity statistics for each care provider. How many patients did I see that month? How many "complex" visits did I bill? How about my colleagues? Discussing these reports at our staff meetings angered me. Were the number of patients seen and the revenue generated the only things that counted? I understood how hard it was to keep clinics like ours afloat and that someone had to pay attention to the bottom line, but I did not want that someone to be me.

Burnout

The EMR transition took months. I was exhausted by the long hours—also, irritable and labile. My previously rare migraines became more common. When I am reminded of this period in my life, for example by writing about this experience, I feel the anxiety return, my gut squeeze, and my heart race. I guess this is a tiny taste of what PTSD feels like. Even worse than my physical symptoms was the turmoil in my mind. My resentment at the clinic continually simmered and sometimes boiled to anger. It seemed like my neurocircuits were stuck, like a vinyl record repeating itself in my head over and over and over…."I am being wronged, it is not fair, I am being wronged, it is not fair." Negative thoughts had hijacked my mind. Later I would come to learn much more about what actually was happening in my mind and my body. But at that time I only recognized that it was unbearable. I begged God for help. Any kind of help. I just wanted the whir of negative thoughts to stop. I wanted to find peace of mind. But I kept on working.

One Sunday in late 2012, while having a family breakfast after Mass, I blew up at my stepdaughter for no reason and, unable to control my inexplicable swirl of anger, I fled the room in tears.

My behavior stunned me. After I calmed down, I reflected on my increasing stress at work and how crummy I felt. I was forced to conclude that my life was out of control. I was burned out. The next day I turned in my six-month notice at work.

Looking Back

The needs of disadvantaged populations, such as those seen at Christ House or CRHS, are vast and deeply rooted—the end results of racism, poverty, lack of education, homelessness, injustice, and war.

Many of our clinic patients immigrated to the United States from El Salvador[26] in the '80s, fleeing from a long and bloody civil war in which the U.S. provided massive military support to the government. More recently, the border war between Eritrea and Ethiopia from 1998-2000 led to many Eritrea immigrants and asylum seekers—and some came to our clinic.

The guys at Christ House were born of another migration, the Great Migration when almost six million African Americans fled the injustices and abuse of the Jim Crow South between 1905 and 1970. Most of those men I described, and William too, were either part of the flux or children of the migrants. If you read *The Warmth of Other Suns: The Epic Story of America's*

---

26. https://www.migrationpolicy.org/article/el-salvador-civil-war-natural-disasters-and-gang-violence-drive-migration

Great Migration[27] by Isabel Wilkerson, you will gain great understanding about what African Americans went through in the last century, part of the legacy of slavery they carry on their backs.

In spite of all this, every day I saw how individuals survived, started over, and thrived even when they had dealt with poverty, war, or injustice their whole lives. I was awed by their resilience, the power of love and respect to help them heal, and the all-encompassing gratitude they so often demonstrated. This impacted me deeply in ways I couldn't fully understand or express.

The extraordinary words of lawyer Bryan Stevenson in *Just Mercy*[28] expressed truths that helped me understand my deep reactions to working in Washington, DC. Stevenson founded the Equal Justice Initiative and has spent his life trying to find justice for the wrongly condemned. Toward the end of his book, he writes about how we are all broken—his clients, the system, himself. He says: "I guess I'd always known but never fully considered that being broken is what makes us human. We all have our reasons....But our brokenness is also the source of our common humanity, the basis for our shared search for comfort, meaning, and healing. Our shared vulnerability and imperfection nurtures and sustains our capacity for compassion. We have a choice. We can embrace our humanness, which means embracing our broken natures and the compassion that remains our best hope for healing." He goes on to say that "...there is a strength, a power even, in understanding brokenness, because embracing our brokenness creates a need

---

27. Isabel Wilkerson, *The Warmth of Other Suns: The Epic Story of America's Great Migration*, (Random House, 2010).
28. Bryan Stevenson, *Just Mercy, Bryan* (One World, 2015), 289, 290.

and desire for mercy, and perhaps a corresponding need to show mercy." It's a privilege for me to share with you this profound message of hope as expressed by Stevenson, who quoted Thomas Merton in his book.

> "As long as we are on earth, the love that unites us will bring us suffering by our very contact with one another, because this love is the resetting of a Body of Broken Bones."

> —Thomas Merton,
> *New Seeds of Contemplation*, p. 72

PART III

Finding the Garden

10

———·•·———

Self-Help

From this point in the book, I will diverge from a straight chronological account of my life in order to better explain how I made sense of my path and put the pieces together to find serenity and health—and how you can do the same. As I found my own path to abundant health, I realized it was much broader than the traditional path I'd been promoting as a doctor. I reflected over the preceding few years and saw how I had experienced firsthand what I had observed so often in the clinic and at Christ House, namely that stress can devastate health because of the complex interplay of mind, body, and spirit. Now I had to take advantage of this interplay in order to heal. Most significantly, I also was realizing the many ways my faith contributed to my well-being. God, the great physician, was definitely walking with me.

My own journey to healing of mind, body, and spirit led me to develop at my church a program called Serenity and Health—designed to help others find their own path to this abundant health. It was self-help in the truest sense

because what I learned from my study and from the participants helped me just as much as it helped the participants.

Before delving in to Serenity and Health, I need to catch
you up on what was happening to my own health in the
lead-up to my 2013 retirement.

Seeking Peace in the Suburbs

By fall of 2010, I was a real mess—very stressed at work and
constantly dwelling on my resentment and anger about
the new EMR system. I pleaded with God to help me find
peace. I begged William to pray for me. In addition to
stresses at work, city living with its congestion and noise
was getting harder for me. A quiet night was rare. And,
there was violence. A man was shot on the sidewalk below
our apartment—I will never forget seeing that yellow crime
scene tape surrounding the entrance to our building. Still,
we had not seriously considered moving.

One Saturday morning after Mass, we joined friends
for breakfast in their new condo in nearby Hyattsville,
Maryland. After breakfast, before heading home, William
and I spontaneously set off on a little drive in a residential
area near our friends' condo. We turned down a street
that said, "No Outlet" and saw a house with a "For Sale
by Owner" sign. We stopped in front of the house and
observed a forest just ahead of us and a park across the
street. I could practically hear God whispering in my ear,
"Here is a house for you in a quiet neighborhood where
you can find peace."

By the end of that year, 2010, we moved from Adams
Morgan in Washington, DC, into that 1952 three-bedroom,
ranch-style home. We did find peace, new friends, and a
garden, although not the solution to all my problems.

When we moved out of the Kairos building to Maryland, we were no longer members of the residential community of Christ House, and I was no longer eligible to work there. My responsibilities at the clinic, however, were unchanged. Whereas before I had a forty-five second walking commute to get to work, now I had a combined walking and metro commute that took nearly an hour. For the first couple of years, I enjoyed this commute and was convinced the additional exercise and living out of the city would help my stress.

Slowing Down

Then I started having problems with walking. The explanation was nothing exotic, just plain old arthritis. Rather than walking, I had to start taking the shuttle bus from the Metro Station to our neighborhood. I learned that the more you worry about your pain, the worse it is. I often thought of my mother who also had arthritis and had her first hip replacement when she was fifty-five years old. I realized I hadn't been very sympathetic. Nor, sadly, had I been there to help her.

I tried exercises, doctors, and physical therapy. The physical therapy was particularly frustrating. My hip exercises hurt my back. My back exercises hurt my knees. I didn't like these changes happening to my body. The physical therapist suggested pool therapy. I was very reluctant. Who would ever want to go swimming for exercise? I swam regularly as a kid, but couldn't imagine swimming for exercise at this point in my life. All I could think about was the wetness, the cold, and the wet hair that would need to be dried and styled afterward. But since I was desperate and had few options, I tried pool therapy at the hospital and was amazed how beneficial it was.

In 2012 I started dragging myself to a nearby community pool at 6:30 a.m. several days a week before work—I didn't have to leave for work until late morning. Initially I couldn't swim even one lap, but with time I gained endurance and found it exhilarating. The pool was full of seniors water walking or swimming for exercise and rehabilitation. Going to this pool was the first major step I had taken to regain my physical health. It was empowering. I hurt less and felt better equipped physically and mentally to deal with the left hip pain, which continued to worsen.

As a doctor, I knew, of course, that pain can negatively impact sleep. Experiencing this was, well, painful. How many times can you wake up in the night seeking just the right position that doesn't hurt? How many pillows can you use to prop yourself up? How many pills can you safely take to relieve the pain? We purchased a memory foam bed, which I was sure would solve my sleep problems. Unfortunately, I was wrong. For the first time in my life I found myself taking ibuprofen daily.

My clinic problem list would have read: osteoarthritis, multiple joints; osteoarthritis, L. hip, severe; migraines; insomnia; osteoporosis; chronic rhinitis. Plus, I was burned-out. Compared to many of my patients, my problem list looked like nothing. But it sure did not feel like nothing. This was my state when I gave my notice at work.

Retirement

I was sixty-four, newly retired, and dealing with health issues. As an adult, the only times I had not worked were three six-week pregnancy leaves, time off during Jacob's illness and after his death, and the few months break as I prepared to start the family medicine residency in 2000. Upon retirement,

I missed being a doctor—no longer seeing patients and trying to help people feel better. I always loved my profession, in spite of my stresses. It is a tremendous honor to have patients trust you with their secrets, their vulnerabilities, and their bodies. I wanted to do something useful. I knew God wanted me to use my gifts and talents, and I kept thinking about different ministries or formats that might work.

But at that moment, the priority for me was to regain my health. My goals were to find peace in my head, to have no pain, to be able to walk, and to sleep. Ten years earlier when I started working in Washington, DC, my health had been good. I ate everything in moderation, including meat, but not much junk food. My weight was normal. I didn't smoke. During my early years in Washington, I walked a lot— for errands, my Spanish lessons down by Dupont Circle, or fun strolls with William to Georgetown and all over the city. I also enjoyed an occasional yoga class. Planned stress-reduction practices were not part of my repertoire. Now I recognized I was far from healthy and needed to find my path to health.

Steps to Serenity and Health

What follows is my description of the origins of the Serenity and Health program, the steps I followed in my recovery, and the benefits to participants—which, of course, are available to you as well. You will see my repeated reference to the interplay between the body, mind, and spirit.

I had seen in the clinic and experienced myself how mind-body-spirit interactions play out. Depression, anxiety, and stress worsen physical symptoms and aggravate diseases. Pain and illness can aggravate depression and anxiety. Spiritual restlessness can cause angst and lack of satisfaction with life. As my hip pain intensified, I had to use a cane. It was humbling and awkward—trying to open a door while carrying a parcel and a cane is difficult and made me feel clumsy. I felt like an old lady—once I was crushed to hear someone refer to me as that gray-haired lady with the cane. My sleep difficulty added to my irritability. The more I worried about my pain and my limited mobility, the worse it felt. One bad thing fed another bad thing to create a downward cycle.

Now that I had more free time, I started trying everything I could think of to recover whole health—aiming to heal my mind, my body, and my restless spirit. The steps for my own recovery provided the seeds for Serenity and Health. It debuted in the fall of 2014 as a six-week, small-group program to help registrants find their own path to peace and healing. Just as I was on my journey seeking serenity, health, and closeness to God, so too were the participants. Organizing the program required me to clarify my thoughts and seek even more answers. I felt privileged to journey with others.

In this process of developing the Serenity and Health program, I read many books and articles, from classics to the latest research. I attended retreats and conferences. I talked to friends and colleagues. I scrutinized my medical experience through a new lens and integrated old and new. I even started to think back to my misery during my first marriage, grimly admitting how much suffering is created by messed-up relationships.

The next three sections are titled **Body**, **Mind**, and **Spirit**. **Body** covers the physical body and our health habits—it relates to what is called lifestyle medicine. **Mind** deals with health issues related to the mind and stress. **Spirit** addresses the role of God and what our faith has to do with our health.

Body

Exercise

I reminded myself of my patients when it came to my pain. I was vexed at the lack of clear answers. My primary doctor referred me to a hip doctor, who referred me to a back doctor, who referred me to the physical therapist, who eventually, in frustration, referred me for aquatic therapy. I just wanted to get rid of my pain and be able to walk. I tried different home exercises, limited walking, and added water walking to the pool laps. The eventual diagnosis was left hip osteoarthritis. After a total hip replacement in early 2014, a year after I retired, my walking improved. But I had to finally accept that my musculoskeletal system is a little delicate—I continued to have intermittent unexplained pain. To reduce my chances of needing medications, injections, and more surgery I have continued to exercise with an evolving routine. I added weight training and received valuable help from a personal trainer for several years. My current routine is walking two to three times a week and doing weight-bearing and resistance exercises at home at least twice a week. I have occasional setbacks with new pains, but just keep modifying my routines. I'm doing well, don't take pain pills, and am convinced exercise has done wonders to improve both my mental and physical health.

You may find, as I did, that you will need to continually adjust your exercise program to accommodate your ever-changing life circumstances, aches and pains, and general health. A few pieces of advice: Don't do the same thing every day, try different types of exercise, find something that you enjoy, and keep at it even if you don't have a specific explanation for your ailments—while, of course, following your doctor's guidance.

Types of exercise include aerobic exercises, resistance training, balance practices, and stretching. Yoga fits into several of these categories. The best type of exercise, however, is the one that you actually do. For many people, walking is the easiest place to begin, but there are many options. For ideas and information about exercise, check out these online free sites.[29] The biggest challenge for most people is finding the will to start and continue an exercise routine. To increase your chances of success, start with an easy goal you're pretty sure you can meet, such as: "I will walk for fifteen minutes three times a week." Succeeding with your first goal will empower you to continue.

Eating

I was resistant to changing my diet. I liked what I ate and my weight was normal. But my pain was telling me I had inflammation in my body. I also had a chronic inflammatory nasal condition that mimicked allergic rhinitis, but wasn't seasonal and didn't respond to allergy medicines. The cause of this ailment is unknown. Some foods, such as green, leafy vegetables, fruits, fatty fish, and nuts, are known to have anti-inflammatory properties. In contrast, foods like red meat and refined carbs contribute to inflammation in the body. I was very familiar with the epidemiological studies showing the health benefits of a vegetarian diet. The lower the meat consumption in a country, the healthier the population. Based on all this, I eliminated red

---

29. https://www.danielplan.com/fitness/
    https://www.sparkpeople.com/resource/fitness.asp
    https://www.cdc.gov/physicalactivity/index.html

meat from my diet. Because of scattered reports of allergy to dairy products causing nasal inflammation I also cut out 90% of dairy products. My nose problem is now 75% better. It is hard to evaluate the effects of stopping red meat, but I am very happy to have done so. I still eat chicken and seafood and have added many more bean and lentil dishes to my diet. I also feel good to be contributing to the health of the environment by not consuming red meat.[30]

In Serenity and Health, I recommend these basic steps for healthy eating:

- Follow the Healthy Eating Plate method,[31] which will guide you as to which and how much of each food group you should eat. Vegetables and fruits make up half the plate, whole grain a quarter, and healthy protein a quarter.

- Eat less meat and learn[32] more about the benefits of a plant-based diet.

- Eat at least five servings of fruits and veggies every day.

- Avoid junk food and soda most of the time.

- Shut your kitchen and stop evening snacking at a time you predetermine. Brush your teeth at this time.

- Avoid diets, find an eating routine you can continue long-term.

30. https://www.nationalgeographic.com/environment/article/commission-report-great-food-transformation-plant-diet-climate-change
31. https://www.hsph.harvard.edu/nutritionsource/healthy-eating-plate/
32. https://www.forksoverknives.com/our-story/

Other

Adequate sleep is vital for health. Exercise, a regular routine, and not eating immediately before bedtime all helped me sleep better. Avoiding screen time in the evening also helps.

In Serenity and Health we spent time talking about habits, motivation, and how to make action plans with specific, clearly defined steps we can take to help us reach our eventual goals. These conversations are crucial because facts, statistics, and recommendations about healthy living are rarely sufficient to move people to change their habits.

Knowing about keystone habits is helpful. In *The Power of Habit*, Charles Duhigg describes keystone habits as those that have the power to start a chain reaction of other habits—that they "shift, dislodge and remake other patterns."[33] Exercise can be a keystone habit. I think the swimming worked like that for me, getting me started exercising. Andrew, who shared his story with our group, provides a dramatic example of exercise as a keystone habit. He had gained weight and developed major health problems. He became seriously depressed and feared he couldn't support his family. After heart surgery, he knew he had to lose weight, but was foundering until he saw an announcement in our parish bulletin about a Christian boot camp. He joined, became a regular at the early morning workout, lost weight, regained his health, and even better, rejuvenated his family and his faith. Several years later, he still attends the boot camp five days a week and has become an active volunteer teacher at our parish.

---

33. Charles Duhigg, *The Power of Habit*, (Random House, 2014), 100-101.

Mind

Understanding stress is key to understanding the connection of the mind to health and well-being. The human stress reaction is a massive cascade of chemical reactions and physiological responses in the body that is set off when the mind recognizes a threat. Acute stress is a reaction to a threat that is temporary—the reaction is protective and brief. Chronic stress is what occurs when stressors are so frequent or continual such that there is no time for the body to recover. It is chronic stress, so common in our modern world, that causes or exacerbates many chronic diseases such as heart disease, high blood pressure, obesity, and diabetes.

Here are the four key points to know about stress:

First, it is when the mind determines that a particular stressor is a threat that the stress reaction occurs. Consider a victim of PTSD who hears a loud noise. Based on his past experience in war, his mind unconsciously interprets the noise as a gunshot, a real threat, and his body instantly registers a stress reaction. In contrast, my mind, having no history of trauma, may well conclude the noise was only a car backfire, and I would experience no stress. An adult who suffered a dog bite as a young child may feel more stress around a big dog than someone never having this trauma. Even if she does not remember being bit, her mind might see the dog as a threat.

Second, it is no easy matter to reprogram our minds in ways that will make us less likely to see threats or react to stressors. Cognitive therapy and learning to reframe how we think about threats can be very helpful in reducing stress. But sometimes the programing is too deep. A PTSD victim may intellectually know the loud noise is a backfire, but that knowledge doesn't eliminate the fear and stress. To learn more about chronic stress and the mind, read *The Body Keeps the Score*, a masterful book written by psychiatrist and researcher Bessel van der Kolk. He describes how trauma in life literally reshapes both the body and the brain, and he explores innovative therapies. Dr. van der Kolk also helped me understand ACEs, Adverse Childhood Events,[34] and how they can affect the mind and body through adulthood. In retrospect, I saw how ACEs may have been a significant factor in causing the poor health outcomes I saw while working in Washington, DC.

Mindfulness is another practice that will help reduce stress. I was beginning to see how frequently I was mindless, too busy up in my head to be aware of the present moment. We cannot become mindful just by deciding to become mindful. Steps that increase mindfulness include breathing practices, meditation, guided body scans, and walking in nature. For personal study, consider the classic *Full Catastrophe Living*, by Jon Kabat-Zinn, developer of the Mindfulness-Based Stress Reduction program, now taught and practiced around the world.

Third, there is an antidote for the human stress reaction. It is called the relaxation response. We can intentionally take steps that will turn off the stress reaction in our body by turning on the relaxation response. This was first described in 1975 by Dr. Herbert Benson based on a landmark study involving meditating monks. A classic and easy method to turn on this relaxation response is deep belly breathing. You can simply practice taking several slow easy breaths at intervals when

---

34. Bessel van der Kolk, *The Body Keeps the Score*, (Penguin Books, 2014), 146-150.

you feel stressed, or you can learn more about various breathing practices.[35]

The fourth point deals with resilience, the ability to adapt to and cope with stress. The more resilient we are, the less we will be affected by stress. Add to your life specific activities and behaviors that are known to build resilience, such as: community, finding a meaning or purpose to your life, faith, hobbies, creative pursuits, nature, music, pets, exercise, volunteering, or a gratitude journal. I found that the more I learned about stress and mindfulness, the more self-aware I became. Practices like breathing, walking, and consciously trying to reframe negative thoughts helped me feel more peaceful.

These topics provoked great interest in the Serenity and Health groups. Mari is a petite, married mother who works in a demanding job in a hospital. She shared her experiences dealing with her work stresses that too often made her feel sad and upset. She became so anxious as others judged her work that her heart raced and she would feel ill, consumed with self-doubts. After learning about deep belly breathing in the class, she started going into the bathroom once or twice a day for a preventative session. She described the practice: standing tall, not looking at the mirror, closing her eyes, letting her arms dangle, and taking several slow, easy breaths. Her body softened and relaxed. She noticed she began to be more aware of her reactions to her supervisor—fast breathing, tight chest, and negative thoughts—and immediately could take a couple of breaths, say a prayer, and relax. After some time, her husband even noticed a difference, commenting that she yelled less.

---

35. https://www.health.harvard.edu/mind-and-mood/relaxation-techniques-breath-control-helps-quell-errant-stress-response

Spirit

I found myself repeatedly turning to God, but in a rather haphazard way. At first, I didn't have a regular spiritual discipline, though I greatly valued my prayers, increasing Mass attendance, spiritual talks with friends and with William, and reading my bilingual Bible. I'm delighted to introduce you to a special book and a specific prayer practice that profoundly changed my spiritual life.

The book is Jean-Pierre de Caussade's *The Sacrament of the Present Moment.*[36] Caussade's words helped me begin to understand mindfulness from a spiritual perspective. I realized that I was close to God when I stayed in the moment, not when I was flooded with worry, resentment, anger, or fear—unpleasant, negative emotions that took me far from God and the moment. It was saying a short prayer frequently throughout the day that helped me return to the moment, to God and to peace—over and over again.

The spiritual practice was Centering Prayer. As I read more about it—especially Father Thomas Keating's books—and felt called to increase my practice, I clearly recognized how I needed to slow down my brain, to embrace silence, and to listen. My body craved those things. Even though sitting in a chair to practice Centering Prayer for a few minutes continued to be very challenging for a long time, this form of prayer has brought me to a deeper faith, to a place of trust and surrender that I didn't know was possible. I will go into much more detail about God-centered mindfulness and Centering Prayer in Chapter 12, where I describe the four stages of my spiritual journey.

---

36. Jean-Pierre de Caussade, translated by Kitty Muggeridge, *The Sacrament of the Present Moment* (Harper Collins, 1996, originally as *Self-Abandonment to Divine Providence*).

I was excited to share Centering Prayer. This idea of receptive prayer, a prayer without words or feelings, was new to me and seemed to have great value. Though I was no expert, I offered Father Keating's explanations and guidelines to the Serenity and Health participants. Jill's words echo what others expressed:

"Above all, the program provided a learning opportunity to truly understand what trusting in the Lord meant; how I am able to place into the Lord's hands, my worries, my suspicions, my weakness, all my negative emotions that kept me from being calm, confident, trusting. The primary tool that transitioned my way of approaching challenges was Centering Prayer. I learned to use this tool every day since then. Not only do I find it easier to manage the onset of stress or anxiety, but I also find a peace that is hard to describe. I've been told that the peace I feel is contagious and in some way, thankfully, it touches others."

Deeper

Following the Serenity and Health path helped me feel better physically, have less stress, and be closer to God. Hearing positive stories of growth and healing from the Serenity and Health participants was gratifying. I was happy. But something else was happening, something that was unexpected and, initially, unwelcome. As I purposefully slowed down and introduced quiet time and more prayer in my day, I found myself bothered by persistent nagging questions about myself and my marriage to Jacob. Sometimes I felt I really didn't know who I was. My research for Serenity and Health had included many psychology topics, such as the role of the family of origin, the influence of our unconscious, and the power of patterns established early in life. I kept reading and thinking about these topics.

In the next two chapters, Chapter 11 and 12, I describe what I learned and experienced when I finally dared to more deeply explore my psyche and my spirit. I hope what I share will help you find the peace and direction that I found.

Looking Back

During this phase of my life, I was curious and open. Open to what I did not know, but I was soon to find out.

11

---•---

Detangling

So many of my past decisions and behaviors didn't make sense. I desperately wanted to understand. I finally admitted that to find answers I would have to explore deeper parts of myself, the frontier I had avoided for decades. This interior part of me, beyond where my conscious and unconscious merge, was scary. I had no idea what I would find, though I hoped to discover what motivated me to do the things I did. I could not think or analyze the facts to get answers. This was not a cognitive exercise where I could study, take the exam, and come up with the solutions. I wasn't at all sure where I was heading, but I knew I was being called to someplace deep and unexplored. I had the feeling it would not be a comfortable journey.

Writing to Discover

It was while I was trying to sort all this out that I suddenly realized I should write a memoir instead of the self-help book I'd been working on for several years. I thought my honest story would be a more persuasive teaching tool.

Maybe I also recognized deep down that writing a memoir would help me find the answers I was seeking.

Author Mary Karr helped me understand memoir writing in her books, *The Liars' Club,* and her bestseller, *The Art of Memoir.* This renowned author taught me that in order to write any kind of a meaningful, authentic memoir, I would have to dig up long-buried truths and try to make sense of them. But how does one go about this? I latched on to Karr's explanation: "In memoir the heart is the brain. It's the Geiger counter you run over memory's landscape looking for precious metals to light up. A psychological self-awareness and faith in the power of truth gives you courage to reveal whatever you unearth, whether you come out looking vain or conniving or hateful or not."[37] Even though I was scared, I thought it was time for me to wield my Geiger counter to look into my life. I was drawn to the Geiger counter analogy because I had experience with Geiger counters—as a radiation oncologist, I had used one to measure radiation exposure.

I created a timeline of my life, spread out on four horizontal pieces of paper all Scotch-taped together. I drew a long line across the papers, marked all the years, and then scribbled the major events of my life along the line. It's unsettling to see your whole life penciled on a timeline that reaches the far end of the fourth paper—and then just ends. The late 1980s and '90s were so crowded that my timeline got jumbled as I squeezed in all the events: several moves, busy high school years, daughters heading off for college, major illnesses of two daughters, grave illness of Jacob with many hospitalizations leading finally to home hospice and

37. Mary Karr, *The Art of Memoir,* (Harper Perennial, 2016), 151.

his death in 1997, traveling to India, and ending in 1999 when I left radiation oncology to transition to primary care. I leaned back in my chair and sighed...a big sigh. It had been so busy during those years.

My Diaries

What if I slowly ran Mary Karr's "Geiger counter" over my timeline to carefully search for deeper truths? What deep "precious metals" would be found? Thinking about this was emotional. In fact, studying my timeline made me cry...so many years and people and events all jumbled together, the pencil scribbles looking so messy and impermanent.

I tried to remember details of what I had thought and felt during all those years. I zeroed in on my younger self, straining to recall details. That is when I remembered my diaries. I hadn't looked at them for years. The next day I headed out to the garage on a search and rescue mission. In the far corner under many boxes, I found the small wooden chest my grandpa had made for me when I was six years old. It always sat next to my bed in my pink ballerina upstairs bedroom and eventually become my "memory chest" that held scrapbooks, yearbooks, mementos, and my diaries. I carted it from Oregon to California to Texas to Chicago to Florida to Washington, DC, and finally to Maryland.

I was yielding to a deep yearning to understand myself—what drove my reactions and decisions back then and now? I asked: "Why am I obsessive about controlling my time?" "Why do I feel I always must be doing something productive?" "Why do I sometimes try to avoid even the most insignificant confrontation?" "Why does my brain prefer overdrive?" "Why do I care so much what other people think?" "Why wasn't my relationship to my mother closer than it was?" and, the most troublesome question of all, "Why did I get engaged to Jacob just six-and-a-half weeks after meeting him?"

My five-year diary was near the top of my chest under an old diploma. It is a three-by-five-inch, burgundy-colored little book with a broken lock. In it I had scrawled brief tidbits of my life during my tenth to fourteenth years. During the years 1965 through 1969, when I was in high school and college, I wrote every day, filling five separate notebooks, one a year. Here I found more detailed and meaningful entries, some of which I've shared earlier in the book.

That same evening I settled down in my office to start reading these five diaries, page by page. Now and then I would stop and stare at the dark window, shocked by the discrepancies between what I remembered and what I was reading. I had "forgotten" about my eating disorder. I had "forgotten" that I had an active social life in college, with plenty of boyfriends and dates. I had "forgotten" I dated other guys during my six-and-a-half-week courtship with Jacob. Sitting alone in my office that fall evening, I learned what cognitive dissonance feels like. It is not some kind of intellectual difference of opinion. It was disconcerting and downright painful. Who was I, anyway? Initially I tried to deal with my distress by sharing details with family and friends. One evening at a neighbor's house, sitting around a table with several other women friends for a birthday gathering, was particularly memorable. I couldn't stop talking as I shared things I'd found...the dating, parties, my eating problems, and my brief courtship while dating other guys....I don't think my friends could recognize the young lady I was describing. After all, I was the educated doctor and proud originator of the Serenity and Health program at church. They were seeing a side of me that was new to them—just as it was new to me.

Therapy

Though I had brief periods of counseling during my first marriage, I had never been interested in therapy. I had repeatedly said that I had no desire to dig for trouble. But now I was starting to think differently.

Within a few days of reading my diaries, in a powerful example of synchronicity or what I prefer to call grace, I was invited to a dinner by Paul and Marge, a couple from church. I didn't know them well, but knew they lived somewhere in our neighborhood and that they were therapists and daily Mass attendees. The dinner in their home turned out to be a gathering of Christian therapists. During that evening, Paul showed me his office and told me a great deal about Internal Family Systems (IFS), a type of therapy that he and Marge sometimes used and found particularly helpful. Every fiber of my body went on high alert—I listened with rapt concentration to his every word. The very next day, after morning Mass, I approached this couple. Just like that…Voila! I had a therapist and my first appointment. Paul's office was a short walk from my home.

IFS is a model of psychotherapy developed by psychologist Richard Schwartz and beautifully described in *Self-Therapy*[38] by Jay Earley. In IFS, the psyche is divided into subpersonalites or parts, each part with its own feelings, perceptions, beliefs, motivations, and memories. The goal of the therapy is to get to know and welcome all of our parts, even those that seem to be causing us harm.

38. Jay Earley, *Self Therapy*, (Pattern System Books, 2009)

Unique descriptions are used in IFS to describe the various parts. Protectors and exiles are two extreme parts that we all have. A protector's role is to shield us from pain. Protectors fill their role in different ways. An abused child might find herself being "protected" for years by her protector-self who learned early on to get relief by shutting down emotions or turning to alcohol. The protector-self keeps on "protecting" even when the original threat is long gone. An exile is very different; it is the part of self still in pain from childhood experiences. These exiles carry painful emotions and negative beliefs into adulthood, such as: "The world is not safe;" "I cannot trust anyone;" "I am not lovable."

I studied IFS and learned the object was to help me know and welcome all my parts with curiosity and compassion. What part of me became convinced as a youth that boys wouldn't like me, despite evidence to the contrary? What part of me knew to the core that my worth totally depended on my work and productivity? What part in me was always afraid to speak my truths—all the way from long ago not being able to tell Jacob I needed more time before getting engaged, to more recently not asking the bakery woman to please wear gloves when she sliced my bread? What part of me couldn't talk to my mom? Even with my own children, why couldn't I talk freely about sex or so many other sensitive topics? What was I afraid of?

Then came my first appointment with Paul. He was influenced by IFS, but also used other systems in his work with me. With his gentle listening and prodding, I was able to re-experience parts of my childhood and youth in such a way that I felt compassion for that little girl who tried to please and excel above all else. In IFS terms, I had distanced myself from my core, my Self, often called the true self. This

Self is described by IFS as our spiritual center. It is relaxed, open, and accepting of oneself and others. "When you are in Self, you are grounded, centered, and non-reactive. You don't get triggered by what people do….When you are in Self, you come from a depth of compassion, enabling you to be loving and caring toward others as well as yourself and your parts. The Self is like the sun—it just shines….It is the agent of psychological healing in IFS."[39]

I slowly started to realize how my exile and protector parts had been taking the lead in my life, rather than my true self—who should have been the leader. These protector parts had long been urging me to keep working and to avoid the pain of any confrontation by ignoring my own desires or needs. My protectors were only doing their job, a role they had learned so well when I was a child—to do anything to protect my exile-self from pain, rejection, or confrontation.

Though the language and practice of IFS initially seemed strange, I saw growth in myself. I was even open to trying Eye Movement Desensitization and Reprocessing or EMDR.[40] This is a psychotherapy treatment originally created to alleviate distress caused by traumatic memories. The rationale is that a client's focus on the external stimulus of eye movements or hand tapping will facilitate accessing emotionally disturbing memories with less distress, and hence, more ability to process these memories. Although I only tried it a few times, I do think it was useful.

A good friend of mind had long been telling me about her therapist, Marian, who uses a type of therapy called Bowen

39. Jay Earley, *Self Therapy*, (Pattern System Books, 2009) 29.
40. Eye Movement Desensitization and Reprocessing. For more information: https://www.emdr.com/what-is-emdr/

Family Systems (BFS)—different from Internal Family Systems (IFS). During a break from seeing Paul, I decided to give Marian a try and learn more about Bowen Family Systems. I dove into the book she recommended, *Extraordinary Relationships, A New Way of Thinking About Human Interactions*[41], by Dr. Roberta M. Gilbert. This turned out to be one of those special books that changed my life. I was primed for a system like this because, in my personal and professional life, I had learned that much suffering is caused by messed up relationships and family issues. Gilbert offers a detailed, case filled, practical presentation of BFS, a system of psychotherapy developed in the '70s by Dr. Murray Bowen. Gilbert describes the three-generational and nuclear family, not the individual, as the emotional unit, and states, "When people live together in a family they tend to pass anxiety and immaturity from one person to another. As anxiety automatically moves in relationship systems, it often does so in well-defined and often-observed ways."[42] She describes four recognized patterns of behavior:

- Conflict
- Distance/cutoff
- Overfunctioning and underfunctioning
- Triangling

The first pattern of behavior is conflict. In 1976, Bowen[43] said, "The basic pattern in conflictual marriages is one in which neither gives in to the other or in which neither

41. Roberta M. Gilbert, *Extraordinary Relationships*, (Leading Systems Press, 2017).
42. Roberta M. Gilbert, *Extraordinary Relationships*, (Leading Systems Press, 2017), 217.
43. Murray Bowen, *Family Therapy in Clinical Practice*, (Jason Aronson, 1978), 377-378. Quoted in *Extraordinary Relationships*, 13.

is capable of an adaptive role....The relationship cycles through periods of intense closeness, conflict that provides a period of emotional distance, and making up, which starts another cycle of intense closeness." This certainly applied to my relationship with Jacob.

The second behavior pattern is distance. Of this, Bowen[44] said, "There is a spectrum of ways spouses deal with fusion [emotional attachment] symptoms. The most universal mechanism is emotional distance from each other. It is present in all marriages to some degree and in a high percentage of marriages to a major degree." Signs of distancing are periods of no communication, workaholism, substance abuse, excessive time on hobbies, or lack of knowledge about or contact with families. Cutoff is the extreme form and is the other side of the coin from fusion—both indicate unresolved emotional intensity. Cutoff and distancing run in families. My family and Jacob's family are no exception. Remember how my family had next-to-no contact with my dad's sister and family living in the same city. Later in life I came to learn of the plight of a sister-in-law of Jacob—her husband didn't talk to her for years. Jacob did not appear to have close relationships with his siblings and other relatives, although there were some striking exceptions. One was the touching and healing moment when his brother and sister, accompanied by his nephew, came from India to donate bone marrow for him. Another was the love and kindness shown to our family by Adam, another nephew, during and after Jacob's death.

One quote[45] from Gilbert's book really hit me: "For whatever reasons, it does seem that, commonly, the American

44. ———, 382. Quoted in *Extraordinary Relationships*, 24.
45. ———, *Extraordinary Relationships*, 35.

way of growing up is to leave home and never return again, emotionally speaking." It is painful to admit it, but this kind of cutoff probably applies to me—at least until now.

The third pattern of behavior is overfunctioning and underfunctioning, also present in my marriage. Why did Jacob not do any housework and participate in a significant way in childcare? Is it possible that I wanted to control the kids and the house and didn't give him space? Maybe Jacob felt I didn't trust him to be in charge of the girls' needs or to buy the correct food if he went grocery shopping by himself. Was I the overfunctioner in this case? Why did I not help out with the home paperwork, the bills, insurance, investments, and car registrations? I thought, maybe incorrectly, that he wanted to do it all. In the home office, Jacob was the overfunctioner.

Gilbert notes that every overfunctioner deserves his underfunctioner, and every underfunctioner deserves his overfunctioner. Each is in a bind. I certainly did not understand any of this at the time. To me, our workload imbalance was very unfair, and I totally blamed him for it. I did have the option to stop overfunctioning, but I never exercised that option for two reasons. First, I wasn't really aware I had a choice. Second, probably unconsciously, I did not want to feel the anxiety and bear the consequences of such a choice. Continuing to overfunction was an easier path than a big fight. If somehow I had been sufficiently self-aware to draw better boundaries and to stop enabling his underfunctioning in the care of the children or house, I'm not sure what would have happened. Or, what if he had insisted I carry part of the responsibility of dealing with our family money matters? This kind of altered pattern probably would have provoked loud protests and then a backsliding to the original pattern, personal growth of both parties, or possibly a break in the relationship.

With this quote, Gilbert shocked me to my very core: "Family systems theory tells us that each partner in an important relationship is exactly as emotionally mature as the other."[46] Really? You have got to be kidding. But she wasn't kidding. I've thought about this a lot. For years I blamed Jacob for everything wrong in our marriage, and this belief protected me from having to face my own issues. I lacked the emotional maturity to do so. Gilbert further says: "The burden of responsibility for one's happiness will not be placed on the other. Rather, responsibility for feeling good or bad, as well as for one's thought and behavior, rests solely with the self."[47] This is challenging stuff.

Finally, the last behavior pattern is triangles. If there is anxiety or problems between two people, they often absorb a third person or new focus, like a project or a dog. A three-sided triangle is more stable than a two-person relationship. It's like the anxiety can be dispersed to the third person. Gilbert says triangles are ubiquitous in relationships. I've heard it said that triangles are the glue that sticks dysfunctional families together. The most difficult triangle in my life was me, Jacob, and my mom. I've also come to understand how I participated in triangles with my daughters. The tragedy of my trip to New Mexico fits into this category, with Serena stepping up to stabilize the situation between Jacob and me.

Unresolved emotional attachments and stresses from childhood become hardwired into these four patterns, only to create sparks and reactivity throughout life. We

---

46. ———, *Extraordinary Relationships*, 44.
47. ———, *Extraordinary Relationships*, 49.

commonly adopt one or more of these four patterns in childhood in order to manage anxiety—these behaviors and attitudes help us deal with the normal stresses and concerns that are part of our growing up years. But when we unconsciously continue these patterns as adults it creates anxiety and grief in relationships. It was humbling to see so many unhealthy patterns from my life clearly described in Gilbert's book.

An important concept is that of fusion. Fusion[48] is the "emotional attachment of two or more selves," with both selves intensely emotionally reactive. It develops if you don't have a strong sense of self or personal boundaries. Fusion occurs when the self is immature, not developed, or in BFS lingo, is not differentiated. "Differentiation of Self[49]" is the key to the whole caboodle. It is roughly similar to emotional maturity, though much broader. People who are more differentiated tend to have happier, healthier, and more successful lives, with less reactivity in their behaviors. They are more emotionally independent and not fused to another. At lower levels of differentiation, people demonstrate behavior patterns that are based on emotion; their choices are more reactive and automatic, presenting as compliance, rebelliousness, fear of rejection, and fear of what others think. A more differentiated adult will see inevitable relationship conflicts as opportunities for growth.

Our level of differentiation is largely influenced in childhood by our parents and grandparents and by their levels of differentiation. Fortunately, though, as adults we can become more differentiated with effort and often with help.

---

48. ———, *Extraordinary Relationships*, 214.
49. ———, *Extraordinary Relationships*, 212.

If we develop our ability to self-observe by practicing mindfulness, we can become more aware when we are thinking and reacting emotionally and automatically. Without this self-awareness, we will continue to mindlessly react rather than mindfully respond to every stressor or awkward encounter that comes our way. In my overfunctioning example, my mindless reaction to Jacob's underfunctioning was continued anger and resentment.

Insights

How in the world can these kinds of ingrained patterns be changed? How can we heal and grow? How can we know and embrace our core self? I believe the answer is "slowly and with concerted effort." I am a work in progress, as those who know me well will readily attest. Learning about mindfulness and trying to practice it is critical. Marian repeatedly asked me to pause and think about my motivation in any kind of stressful circumstance, or, in other words, to be mindful. Was I starting to feel anxiety and tightness in my chest and starting to prattle on about nothing in a stressful conversation? Why? What was the trigger? Did I expect the other person to have the same opinion as me? Was I worrying because I thought my solution was better than his or that he might think badly of me? Did I want my daughter to call more often or do a specific thing because I just knew it would be best for her, or, was it really because I was anxious and needed to have my needs filled? Maybe I was just a hovering mother not trusting my adult daughter to know when and what she needed for herself? Could it really be all about me—wanting the other person to do such and such in order that I would feel better, look better, worry less, and so on?

How many choices and decisions have I made during my life primarily to ease the anxiety I felt? I understand now that many of my choices and decisions were powerfully influenced by unconscious imprints from childhood. My parents were great parents, and they did not abuse or traumatize me. Yet, they, like all parents, were imperfect. Plus, I was a child and had an immature lens on life—so my brain sometimes retained a distorted version of what I had learned from my parents or other life experiences. Those "personalized" versions are still stored deep in my psyche and are the imprints that continue to influence my thinking and behavior. I can now recognize two problematic patterns, that is, the low-resistance paths I've often followed to manage anxiety.

The first was the path of agreeability. If I agreed with the plan or idea of the other person, I could avoid any conflict and, hence, avoid any anxiety. Examples are my acquiescing to Jacob's wishes rather than facing the anxiety of confrontation and maybe even rejection. My true self was not speaking when I said I would transfer colleges the last semester or when I said we could skip the family dinner after our wedding or even when I said yes to a marriage proposal after six-and-a-half weeks. I always thought I was just being nice, agreeable, giving, or loving. In reality, I just didn't know my true self well enough to know what I really needed or wanted. Of course, I couldn't always be nice and agreeable—sometimes, after denying my true feelings for too long, they would either leak out in passive-aggressive behavior or explode in anger.

The second low-resistance path was to always work and be productive—and too often to overfunction. This path is complicated. It has served me well in life because I've accomplished a lot. Being productive and efficient helped me get through some very busy times. But this drive so controlled me that I never thought I had a choice. I was working and away so much when my children were little. Six weeks for my maternity leaves—I thought I didn't have options. The reality was I couldn't deal with the presumed negative reactions of my male colleagues if I took more time or with the sense of failure or quitting I would personally feel if I somehow adjusted my work hours. I deeply regret not giving my daughters more of my time and attention when they were little. I have become more aware of this loss for them and for me as I have watched how much time my daughters lavish on their children.

Writing this book and working with a therapist helped me see how these two paths contributed to my difficulties in my marriage and raising a family. Therapy also has helped me fully accept that I did the best I could, as did Jacob. My faith also helps me handle the guilt that sometimes still nags me.

One thing I don't fully understand. I am still uncomfortable with the fact that I didn't feel that close to my mom, or to my dad either—even though I know they loved me deeply. Since I likely copied my mom's style of loving, this influenced my own mothering in ways I've been slow to understand. As I said before, I am most definitely a work in progress.

I want to always remember one of Marian's maxims: "Never underestimate the power of a non-anxious presence." If I can remain calm, centered, and without anxiety in a stressful encounter or circumstance, my peace will be felt by others. It is contagious. What a tremendous potential to heal a relationship or family.

Personal Study

Let me mention some other books that were particularly helpful to me. At the top of the list is M. Scott Peck's 1978 classic, *The Road Less Traveled*, which I have read multiple times. Peck, a psychiatrist, based his work on two assumptions: First, there is no distinction between the mind and the spirit; hence, there is no distinction between the process of achieving spiritual growth and achieving mental growth; second, "...this process is a complex, arduous and lifelong task."[50] The way he linked spiritual and emotional health was new to me, but it made so much sense.

Rev. Pete Scazzero and his wife, Geri, have a similar approach. In their respective books, *Emotionally Healthy Spirituality* and *The Emotionally Healthy Woman, Eight Things You Have to Quit to Change Your Life,* they reveal the struggles they faced in their marriage and go on to discuss how it is impossible to be spiritually mature while remaining emotionally immature. Geri and Pete are courageously honest as they describe their difficulties—and joyful as they share their path to emotional and spiritual maturity.

Looking Back

Seeking emotional health, differentiation, a higher level of consciousness, maturity, greater self-awareness—or whatever you choose to call it—is challenging. It is not a defined cognitive process that one can accomplish by following a step 1-2-3 guidebook. It was so strange to sit with Paul and begin to grasp that I could not just think or plan a way to the answers and understanding I was seeking. Instead I had to be open to allow the process

---

50. M. Scott Peck, *The Road Less Traveled*, (Simon and Schuster, 1978.)12.

to happen. It was in that learning to "be" rather than to "do" that I started to be aware of changes in my perceptions. I'm convinced that my Centering Prayer meditative prayer practice, which I embraced as precious time resting with my Lord, actually had already altered my mind, quieting it, and making it more open to therapy. It's like my emotional mind was evolving from a hard, scratchy, dried-up, old sponge to a soft, expanding sponge that was increasingly able to absorb water. The process started slowly. Initially the dry and dull sponge repelled the water, but it gradually became more pleasant to touch and was flexible—less likely to crack when pressure was applied. My mind was becoming more permeable to challenging memories, perceptions, and ideas. As I became more mindful, I became more aware of my suffering or anxiety in a way that helped me to meaningfully respond instead of automatically reacting to my distress.

The path to growth and differentiation requires each of us to be fully aware of our suffering and our pain, including that which we carry from our parents and grandparents. Our challenge is that we are programmed to avoid that suffering. We don't like to suffer. Rather than face it, we sometimes deny it. We also have many rationalizations saying, "It's really not that bad" or convincing ourselves it is the good, kind, or Christian path. Alternatively, we can distract ourselves from the pain with work or numb ourselves with alcohol, drugs, or any addictive habit. Honestly admitting to and facing the pain is the first step to change and growth. When we finally accept that the pain we are experiencing is worse than any pain or anxiety that might come from change, we are ready to take our first step toward change and personal growth. My moment was my

"Abraham experience," my first step to a different way of living my life.

Mary Karr writes sharply about what she calls "Blind Spots and False Selves," saying "...anybody maladroit at apology or changing her mind just isn't bent for the fluid psychologic state that makes truth discoverable." She goes on to say, "No matter how much you're gunning for truth, the human ego is also a stealthy, low-crawling bastard, and for pretty much everybody, getting used to who you are is a lifelong spiritual struggle."[51]

The Skin Horse in *The Velveteen Rabbit* said it best:

> "It doesn't happen all at once," said the Skin Horse. "You become. It takes a long time. That's why it doesn't happen often to people who break easily, or have sharp edges, or who have to be carefully kept. Generally, by the time you are Real, most of your hair has been loved off, and your eyes drop out and you get loose in the joints and very shabby. But these things don't matter at all, because once you are Real you can't be ugly, except to people who don't understand."[52]

As I became more accepting of my failures and foibles, I found myself being more accepting of the failings and limitations of others. William and I joke about one key to our strong relationship: We fully accept that we are both really messed up, but at the same time, trust that each of us is trying to do better every single day.

51. ——, *The Art of Memoir*, (Harper Perennial, 2016), 152-3.
52. Margery Williams Bianco, (*The Velveteen Rabbit*, 1922).

What about you? Have you suffered with difficult relationships? I hope my story gives you some ideas on how you can better understand yourself, your motivations, and your anxieties—only then can you move in a healthy direction. It's not easy and you might need help, either with personal study (see resources in the appendix) or therapy. But it will be worth it.

Struggling to write this memoir has helped me get to know my true self. I now understand this journey of self-discovery will continue until I die. The part of this process that thrills me is gradually understanding how it aligns with my spiritual journey.

12

·•·

Faint Gleam of Heaven

Even though I was aware that spiritual writers, like psychologists, speak of true self and false self, I glossed over this. I didn't understand how knowing my true self and knowing God were linked—and I didn't try to understand. The faith of my youth seemed sufficient. What follows is a description of my faith journey divided into four stages, followed by a discussion of true self and false self. I'm hoping that reading my story will stir you to reflect on your own spiritual journey. Ask yourself whether you are following your path or God's path.

Stage 1: Early Religious Education

I attended Catholic school from first grade through high school. Since my family did not talk about God or pray together, my early beliefs about God and faith came from my Catholic schools and our Catholic church. The dedicated Dominican nuns and lay teachers taught us about Jesus, the Bible, prayer, the sacraments, and so much more. During the early years we studied to prepare for our first sacraments: Penance (also known as Confession or the

Sacrament of Reconciliation) and Holy Communion. In eighth grade we received Confirmation. I can recall little about how I felt when I received these sacraments. During these years we attended Mass daily with our classmates. It would take decades for me to return to daily Mass and fully appreciate this gift of receiving Jesus in Communion.

We spent a great deal of time studying and memorizing parts of the *Baltimore Catechism*,[53] the official book of Catholic doctrine and widely used in Catholic schools until the late '60s. Sin was a big topic. I still have my original *Baltimore Catechism*, and it says this about mortal sin, the most serious type of sin: "Mortal sin is a grievous offense against the law of God." It goes on to describe how mortal sin deprives the sinner of sanctifying grace and "makes the soul an enemy of God, takes away the merit of all its good actions, deprives it of the right to everlasting happiness in heaven, and makes it deserving of everlasting punishment in hell." Yikes. Of course, for all these bad things to happen three things are necessary: "First, the thought, desire, word, action, or omission must be seriously wrong or considered seriously wrong; second, the sinner must be mindful of the serious wrong; and, third, the sinner must fully consent to it." It was scary stuff. My young brain processed all I heard about sin, and the takeaway I most remember is that I had to follow all the rules and avoid sin so I could go to heaven. It would take many years for me to realize I did not need to save myself, that I was already saved.

One time in grade school, my girlfriend frantically dashed up to me after she had gone to Confession. She nervously whispered in my ear that Father had told her that

---

53. Ellamay Horan, *Official Revised Baltimore Catechism, Number Two*, (W.H. Sadlier, Inc., 1945).

she and I had committed a mortal sin. She was referring to a loud and silly half-naked dance game she and I had played the previous weekend—which she had felt compelled to confess to the priest. I can hardly recall what happened next, but I think I also ran to the confessional, feeling scared and confused—but nothing like I thought a mortal sinner should feel. My girlfriend and I recently pooled our memories of this episode and had a good laugh about it—though I think it's more sad than funny.

I'm certain the kind nuns emphasized God's unconditional love and his great mercy when they spoke of sin, but this message did not sink in. The result was a kind of performance anxiety and guilt about sin that lingers still. In high school we took a religion class every day, but again, I do not recall much. I think it covered the history of religion and must have been where we repeatedly were taught that Catholic girls do not have sex before marriage. During the years I lived at home, I went to Sunday Mass with my mom and brothers or to a separate Mass to play the organ, but I don't think I spent much time praying on my own.

I think my religious education would have been different if it had occurred a decade later. That's because from 1962-65 the Catholic Church had its famous worldwide doctrinal conference, known as Vatican II. Following this council, the church made significant changes: celebrating Mass in English instead of Latin; encouraging involvement of lay people and especially women in the church; and, increasing the emphasis on the Bible, ecumenism, and social justice. The Holy Spirit was blowing fresh air into the church. But this process took time, and, since I graduated high school in 1967, I did not feel those winds of renewal.

Trying to remember the early steps on our spiritual journeys is a valuable exercise. Ask yourself if you are mindlessly following your childhood path or if you have made an adult commitment to your God and faith.

Stage 2: Faith on Hold

From the time I entered college, I became too busy for a regular practice of my faith. During the years that followed, I wed in a Catholic service, completed medical school, had three children, and worked full-time. I never consciously decided I wasn't a Catholic or a Christian. But gradually I just went to Mass less and less frequently and rarely prayed. I don't remember missing my faith or God during these years. Our two older girls were both baptized when very young, neither in a church, but the youngest was not baptized until later. Our three daughters had scant religious instruction during their early years.

Perhaps you are in some stage similar to this. This faithless period can last forever or it can serve as a transition from a childhood faith to a deeply committed adult faith. It is your choice.

Stage 3: Surrender

In my late thirties, I became increasingly unhappy in my marriage. The pain drove me to seek relief. I wrote in Chapter 4 how I started reading, studying, and praying. Reading C.S. Lewis was like opening the blinds and being flooded with light so brilliant that it was both illuminating and uncomfortable. His explanations and questions made me realize two things: First, that it was and always will be my choice to believe or not to believe; and, second, if I did accept Jesus as my Lord and Savior, I would need to give up control. I would need to say, and mean, the words of Luke 22:42: "...not my will but yours be done." Over time I reached a decision, and it was "yes." I did believe in Jesus and accepted all that this meant, including doing the best I could with the "Not my will, but yours" part.

Eventually, I found my way back to the Catholic Church. It was the comfortable faith of my childhood, and I believed it had been founded by Jesus. I could joyfully worship in this community, enjoy traditions and customs I knew, and celebrate the sacraments, especially Holy Communion, the linchpin of the Mass. I accepted the core teachings of the Catholic Church, though I admit to continuing reservations regarding LGBT issues, divorce, the celibacy requirement for priests, women's issues, and birth control. On these subjects, I continue to pray and ask Jesus to guide me.

You may follow a different path. Our religious experiences vary widely. But I believe if you turn to Jesus and really listen, you will hear clues and know how to proceed. I read that religion is a bridge that leads to God, and we have to be careful not to be more attached to the bridge than the destination. I trust that our Creator God will figure a way to welcome all who try their best to love and serve him, regardless of their religion or faith.

Finding a church was just the beginning of this stage. As my marriage difficulties heated up, I turned more and more to God for guidance and help. I sought spiritual direction with our pastor and other wise Christians I met. I read more and cried my way through *The Seven Storey Mountain* by Thomas Merton. Somehow seeing how much a holy and wise man had suffered on his own journey touched me so deeply it made me cry—I wasn't the only one who suffered while trying to find and follow God's will.

Still miserable and without a direction in my personal life, I started lashing out at God and my husband. The pressure kept growing in our family. I could not contain my sense of desperation. I did believe in God, but had not really relinquished control of my life to him. I remained fully in charge, clutching my anguish…until I finally let go and surrendered my marriage and my children to God, in what I call my Abraham experience. You may recall that there were three events that spurred my decision to stay married. Unlike Abraham, I did not hear a voice from heaven with explicit instructions. I interpreted these three events as a communication from God telling me to cancel my divorce plans. I did that—but I was still worried about the girls. It's clear that at first I didn't fully trust God with my daughters because I continued to demand that he take care of them and protect them from strife in our home. It took time and prayer for me to more fully trust God with my daughters and with my life. I now understand this surrender to God is a journey of a lifetime.

I'm not sure if this was my "dark night of the soul,"[54] but I know it was very dark. If you are in a dark time of your life, just keep praying and looking for the light—sometimes it's easier to see light from a dark place. God is there, waiting.

Stage 4: Growth

Within a few years of my Abraham experience, Jacob was diagnosed with leukemia. Helping in his care and waiting with him in hospitals and the bone marrow transplant unit stirred my soul—God seemed very present. When Jacob died, I had no deep understanding or insights about God's plan or specific meaning I should take from his death. I

---

54. Based on a sixteenth century poem by Spanish mystic and poet St. John of the Cross.

prayed, and believed, that Jacob would find peace, and I grieved a complicated grief.

It was a busy time. Our daughters all left for college, I moved, and I changed medical specialties. I remained active at my parish and, after Jacob's death, joined a small faith group and had my first taste of sharing with other journeying Christians. I did some volunteer work visiting the sick. My prayer life was slowly developing. After starting my new job in Washington, DC, I was greatly influenced by working in the inner city with immigrants and the homeless and by the Christ House community of selfless Christians. It was my first experience facing social justice issues and being introduced to liberation theology, a movement connecting the gospel of Jesus to social and political programs for the poor and oppressed.

Another big change in my life was William. He and I grew to deeply love each other. I learned he is a man with very deep, uncomplicated faith who finds it much easier than me to just go with the flow and trust the Lord. Since our 2006 marriage, we have continued to share our spiritual lives and support each other as "God-buddies." I am very grateful to God for sending William to me.

The need to commit to a spiritual discipline was becoming clear. I started devoting some regular time at home to prayer and scripture. A daily meditation with the Bible readings from the Mass of that day became part of my routine. The Prayer of St. Francis became a favorite. Early on I memorized it and began praying it daily, along with my other favorites.[55]

Those years in Washington, DC, provided a cornucopia of spiritual blessings and challenges. The needs of my

---

55. See Appendix III, Favorite Prayers.

patients were great. I was inspired by the generous spirit of other staff members. I was fortunate to have both informal and formal spiritual direction: informal with William and the Christ House residential community and our weekly meetings; formal with a dear priest who helped me find my bearings as I dealt with the stresses and challenges of seeing so much need and also with the emotional fluster I was experiencing as I fell more deeply in love with William, a man so different than me.

During my season of stress and eventual burnout, I turned more and more to God and was led to two forms of private prayer: 1) the practice of praying in the moment; and 2) the meditative prayer known as Centering Prayer. These two practices transformed my spiritual life. Though they developed in a gradual and interwoven process, I will describe them to you one at a time and with enough detail so you can try the practices if you desire.

Praying in the Moment

When I saw the title, *Sacrament of the Present Moment,*[56] I knew I needed to read this book. My head was whirring with worries and upsets, and I was often far from the present moment. The author, Jean-Pierre de Caussade, a French Jesuit priest during the early eighteenth century, wrote many letters of spiritual direction that were later published in this beloved classic. He describes the simple path to God, calling for an intention to be open to God's will and divine action each moment.

---

56. Jean-Pierre de Caussade, translated by Kitty Muggeridge, *The Sacrament of the Present Moment* (Harper Collins, 1996, originally as *Self-Abandonment to Divine Providence*).

De Caussade gently and lovingly calls us to the simple practice of celebrating each moment with God, as we stay open to his will—knowing that he asks for nothing more. This is a state of mind in which we first surrender our will to God, and then strive to be open to God's divine action, moment by moment, as we trust the outcomes to him. I encourage you to read this special book—you may find yourself praying your way through it, as happened with me.

The overlap of de Caussade's teaching with mindfulness gradually became obvious to me. Mindfulness, a moment-to-moment, nonjudgmental awareness, is a critical tool that can help us respond to stressors instead of mindlessly reacting to them. As a Christian, I used de Caussade's way to create for myself a God-centered mindfulness, and this helped me pray throughout the day.

To understand how this works, we must first acknowledge that we all spend a great deal of time up in our heads thinking, brooding, or worrying instead of paying attention to what we actually are "doing" at that moment, whether it be reading, playing with a child, listening, or even praying. During my burnout, I was full of anger and resentment and found it very difficult to stay in the moment. I know I'm not alone—I think at some time or another we all judge, resent, compare, regret, covet, worry…and more.

Learning to recognize and control or rechannel these negative thoughts can bring us back to the present moment, which also can be described as our center, the place of peace where God resides, or as de Caussade eloquently describes it, the "Sacrament of the Present Moment." Praying throughout the day can help accomplish this. This type of on-the-go prayer has been around for millennia. One example is the Jesus Prayer: "Lord Jesus Christ, Son of God, have mercy on me, a sinner," a prayer with roots in early Eastern Christianity.

I selected a specific, brief prayer that appealed to me, wrote it down, memorized it, and then said it often, adding it to my formal prayer. My words are "My Lord and My God," the words of the Apostle Thomas from John 20:28. I tried to remember to also say it during the day, like when I was grateful for avoiding a car accident or when I saw a breathtaking moon. Sometimes I would think of it after getting aggravated or losing my patience, but gradually I found myself remembering to say it more often and more quickly when I first started to be aware I was feeling stressed. Soon I was astonished to see how the prayer would just pop into my mind if I was starting to get upset, judgmental, anxious, or guilty about the past, present, or future—but also if I felt a surge of gratitude or compassion.

By saying this prayer often, it became a habit. I learned to turn back to God over and over during the day by saying these words. If you try this and commit to developing this habit, you will be amazed how easily it becomes automatic. As this practice became established in my life, I found myself saying "My Lord and My God" dozens, maybe even hundreds of times a day. For the first time, I started to understand what St. Paul might have meant in Thessalonians 5:17 when he advised we pray without ceasing. In her classic work, *Thoughts Matter, The Practice of the Spiritual Life*, Sister Mary Margaret Funk says: "Ceaseless prayer is to continuously breathe the Jesus Prayer or another prayer so that the prayer acts like a mantra always working on one's consciousness at a deeper level for the sake of union with God."[57]

---

57. Mary Margaret Funk, *Thoughts Matter, the Practice of the Spiritual Life*, (Continuum, 2004), 138.

A bonus is that this type of on-the-go prayer reduces stress and, hence, improves health. If I notice I am starting to feel stress, that my voice is getting louder and my chest tighter…I say in my head "My Lord and My God." This mindful pause with my Lord reminds me to take a few deep breaths and start over, thereby deflating the stress response in my body. Or, when I catch myself mindlessly digging into a bag of chips, the words "My Lord and My God" just pop into my brain—I once again pause and ask myself if I really want to eat all those chips.

God-centered mindfulness and my praying in the moment have dramatically changed my relationship with God. I am not exaggerating when I say the experience has been transformational. You may already have your own practice that is similar to this, but if you do not, please try it. You will not be sorry.

Centering Prayer

My study of stress, the relaxation response, and stress reduction led me headlong into the subject of meditation. I visualized a man with white hair, wearing loose, white clothes, sitting lotus-style, fingers in the Chin Mudra position gently resting on the knees, with eastern music in the background. I kept reading about seekers over the centuries who had relied on various meditation practices for peace and transformation. Then I read about the newer research and documented health benefits.[58] Though I was intrigued by meditation, it just didn't feel right. I couldn't connect it to my faith—and the health and peace-of-mind benefits were not enough to make me want to spend my precious time meditating. One

---

58. Daniel Goleman, Richard Davidson, *Altered Traits* (Avery, Penguin Random House, 2017).

day I shared this dilemma with my daughter Sophia, a seeker and meditator. She said, "Mom, why don't you try Centering Prayer?" Even though I had a good friend who had practiced Centering Prayer for years, it had never interested me, and I knew next to nothing about it.

Centering Prayer is meditative prayer, sometimes described as precontemplative. It is receptive prayer without words, emotions, or planned thoughts. The Christian contemplative tradition is rich and long, starting with the Desert Fathers in the third and fourth centuries A.D. and continuing with St. Augustine in the fifth century. St. Bernard, St. Hildegard, Meister Eckhart and Julian of Norwich followed in the Middle Ages. Later came St. Teresa of Avila, St. John of the Cross and, in the twentieth century, Thomas Merton, Basil Pennington, Thomas Keating, and Richard Rohr. Keating and Pennington, in particular, wrote about this rich contemplative tradition in ways that made it accessible to all Christians, not just to monks.

Keating says: "Centering Prayer is not just a method. It is true prayer at the same time, a prayer of consenting to God's presence and action within. Its primary scriptural basis is Jesus' wisdom saying in Matthew 6:6: 'If you want to pray, enter your room, shut the door, and pray to our Father who is in secret, and your Father, who sees in secret, will reward you.' "[59] This becomes an invitation to interior silence and openness to the in-dwelling of the Divine. You can read the official Guidelines for Centering Prayer[60] in the appendix. But let me describe what I do.

When I am at home I do my Centering Prayer in my recliner in the corner of my bedroom, usually twice a day. I

---

59. Thomas Keating, *Open Mind, Open Heart (Bloomsbury, 2006).* 19
60. ——, *Open Mind, Open Heart* (Bloomsbury, 2006), 177.

set an alarm to be sure I have time to do this prayer practice in the morning before other activities. I use an application on my phone called Centering Prayer; it has a timer with gongs, as well as supplemental information and prayers. Twenty minutes is recommended, but you choose. I have chosen the word "Jesus" as my sacred word, what Keating calls an anchor. I settle into my chair, close my eyes, say my word "Jesus" to remind me of my intention to say "yes" to the presence and action of God. I surrender to God this period of prayer. I take easy breaths in and out and add my silent "Jesus" at the start of every in-breath or when I find myself distracted. When thoughts, feelings, discomforts, or noises in the room come into consciousness, which they always do, I just let them float on by and try not to think about them or criticize myself for having them. I just let them go.

Keating asserts that the hardest part of Centering Prayer is actually just sitting down to do it—making the decision and then doing it.

Do not expect results. Do not grade how well you did or count how many distractions or wanderings occurred. I realized all I had to do was to sit down, state my prayer intention, and then wait in silence. The rest is out of my hands. When I started learning about and practicing Centering Prayer, it was impossible to just sit down and do nothing for two minutes, much less the suggested twenty minutes. My mind wandered even faster and further. It seemed such a waste of time. I was still having problems surrendering my time because I was always anxious to be efficient and productive—lists and schedules ruled my life. I couldn't comprehend how William could do "nothing" while he relaxed listening to music. Or, how he could just sit outside and be content for an hour watching the birds, squirrels, or airplanes. If I wanted to relax, it meant I must also occupy myself with a book, my phone, or a conversation. I had been programmed to "do," and found it most uncomfortable to just "be." The result of this was that surrendering my time to just "be" with God in Centering Prayer was very challenging. But I kept at it, comforted by Keating's advice that one couldn't fail at this—as long as you sat there, you were doing it. I learned the key was to keep coming back to my sacred word and to God each time my mind wandered off—gently and without recrimination.

It was as though God had once again leaned close to me, this time whispering in my ear: "Donna, your mind is way too busy thinking, planning, and wandering—and I've noticed you are obsessed with controlling every minute of your day. Come rest with me." I am so grateful that I listened.

My Centering Prayer helped me to appreciate that trusting God with my precious time was key. When I surrendered twenty minutes of my time to God to pray, it meant I would have twenty minutes less to write this book, make the phone calls I needed to make, or cook dinner. By trusting God with this time and the tasks left undone on my list, I was exercising my trust muscle, so to speak, and building more trust in my God. I was saying "Yes" to God over and over and over again. Like reps in the gym.

True Self and False Self

Let me share with you what true self and false self mean, as best I understand. God gave each of us the gift of a true self, defined by Keating as: "The image of God in which every human being is created; our participation in the divine life manifested in our uniqueness."[61] As children, though, we learn to identify instead with our false self, an identity we create to help us cope with the emotional trauma of early childhood. This emotional trauma can arise from neglect and abuse, but it is also experienced by all children just because their parents were not perfect. Early on we learn and repeat the behaviors that win us the most approval and affection—and we hold on to these behaviors as adults even if they don't serve us well. I learned to work hard—and always felt compelled to do that even if it meant neglecting other needs. We also can learn to suppress our emotions, to always be the agreeable helper, or that our worth depends on our performance, looks, or money. When we carry those imprints into adulthood and unconsciously continue to identify with these values, we are living as our false selves.[62]

I was drawn to what Keating said in *Intimacy With God* in the wonderfully titled chapter Divine Therapy. He explains:

"The gospel invites us to recognize that the false self is a disease than can be healed and to accept Christ as the divine physician or, in the context of this paradigm, the Divine Therapist. The healing process is primarily the work of contemplative prayer, which, along with the homework of daily life, constitutes the Divine Therapy."[63]

The interior silence and deep peace that result from a meditative prayer practice soften us and release our emotional blocks and give us insights to the darker side of our personality and our false selves that previously had

61. ——, Invitation to Love, (Continuum, 2010)148.
62. ——, Invitation to Love, (Continuum, 2010), 145.
63. ——, Intimacy with God, (Crossroad Publishing, 2012), 42.

been submerged in our unconscious. About this process, Pennington said:

"Unfortunately, in seeing ourselves as we truly are, not all that we see is beautiful and attractive. This is undoubtedly part of the reason we flee silence. We do not want to be confronted with our hypocrisy, our phoniness. We see how false and fragile is the false self we project. We have to go through this painful experience to come to our true self."[64]

I was starting to see that my "psychological" and "spiritual" paths to healing were merging. Neither was easy, and, as described beautifully in a slim book called *The Gift of Being Yourself,* they are probably one and the same path. The author, David G. Benner, writes "There is no deep knowing of God without a deep knowing of self, and no deep knowing of self without a deep knowing of God."[65]

C.S. Lewis referred to the moment when you think you see that the "first faint gleam of Heaven is already inside you."[66] I think this gleam must come from the embrace of God and my true self. Now that I've seen that gleam, I plan to stay the course until I see the bright light—and finally understand all that is now partially in the shadows.

A Big Garden

I have one more special prayer to share. Years ago I started asking God to help me "stand up tall, smile, and listen." I had learned about the positive psychology of standing tall and smiling. I had also realized I needed help to become a better listener. I cannot even recall how I started saying this prayer

---

64. Https://friendsofsilence.net/quote/author/m-basil-pennington. Friends of Silence Newsletter/Blog, Nov. 2011. https://www.azquotes.com/citation/quote/1054949
65. David G. Benner, *The Gift of Being Yourself* (InterVarsity Press, Expanded Edition, 2015), 22.
66. C.S. Lewis, *Mere Christianity.*

every day. When I said the words, I would automatically sit up straighter, look up to the heavens, smile, and take a slow breath. It made me feel good. After praying it regularly for several years, one day the words stopped me short and made me laugh aloud in joy. I suddenly realized that my S, S and L prayer, for stand, smile, and listen, contained the initials of my three daughters: Serena, Sophia, and Leah.

I realize you probably already have your own disciplines, favorite prayers, traditions or ministries. Christians have a rich treasury to draw on. We are so different from one another, even though we all accept Jesus as our Savior. What speaks to you? Praying or studying the Bible, sacred music, worshipping in church, attending Mass, small faith groups, formal prayers during the day, saying the rosary, charismatic prayer, some form of Christian meditation, silent retreats, caring for the poor or sick, promoting peace and justice, or, most likely, a combination? We are fortunate to have so many different spiritual practices available to us, a beautiful garden of flowers from which we can choose. What kind of bouquet will you create to serve and honor God?

One Word

If I had to pick one word to stand for my spiritual journey it would be trust. Little by little, I was able to trust God more and more. First, I had to trust him with my marriage and my daughters. Then with my husband's illness. After that, I started to trust him with my time and many day-to-day decisions. I pray that one day I can fully trust him with absolutely everything, with my complete will. I realize it is by letting go of every iota of my control that I will be fully free and finally able to love selflessly.

Looking Back

Now you know my spiritual journey as best I can reconstruct it. The view from where I am now is less complicated than it used to be. I believe in God. I love Jesus and want to love like him. I try to trust God with everything. I know he loves me unconditionally and mercifully forgives my failings. All I must do is give him time and space in my life and try to follow his holy will in all things—as best I can understand what that means. That's all there is to it. There is much I don't understand, but I'm fine with that.

What about you? Pray to know God's will and, while you wait, experience how silence, listening, and staying in the moment will lead you to your true self and to God.

13

Paradise

The garden is quiet as I bend close to a rose to take in its fragrance and study the deep red lips of otherwise creamy white petals. I stand up and take a deep breath and enjoy a feeling of peace and joy. I embrace this day and my future with equanimity and hope. I laugh more, hurry less, and listen more attentively than I used to. I know my path, the direction I am going, and the destination. Knowing I am deeply loved by my God has freed me to be myself and love myself, and, thankfully, to be able to love others more fully. This knowledge also spurs me to better care for my body and mind so I can live to the fullest for as many years as I am allotted.

A few concepts are key to my journey and my message to you.

Oneness

My original medical training focused on the body. Early in my career I was impressed by the incredible resilience of my cancer patients and their families. But I didn't fully grasp the connections of mind, body, and spirit until later.

Suffering in my marriage and working in the clinic and Christ House in Washington, DC, slowly opened my eyes and my heart. These experiences and observations led me to more deeply understand how stress and emotional suffering could ravage health and how faith, love, respect, and hope could renew it.

Each of us is made of a body, mind, and spirit bound together into one being. What affects one of the three parts impacts the other parts. Understanding these interactions and that God is the core has been critical to my path and helped me understand how my efforts to be healthy and happy connect with my desire to be close to God—and even one with my God. To help you visualize in a graphic way how this works, I offer an analogy.

The Rope

If you are climbing a mountain or being rescued after falling into a ravine, your life may well depend on the rope being used. For decades, most mountaineers, rescuers, and sailors have used the same type, known as a kernmantle rope. In 1953 the Austrian company Edelweiss revolutionized mountaineering with its introduction of the first kernmantle rope, an innovation that far outperformed other kinds of rope. The kernmantle rope has a unique design consisting of a core (German "kern") and an exterior sheath (German "mantle"). The core is made of twisted fibers that provide most of the tensile strength. The sheath is made of three tightly braided fibers that enwrap and protect the rope from abrasion.

The end result is a rope that is remarkably strong, durable, and flexible. It's less likely to twist, tangle, and fray than a conventional rope. This rope, which is usually constructed with nylon fibers, is described as a "survivalist" rope that is ideal for use as a lifeline.

Let each of us now envision our own lifeline. Consider this special rope to represent your being and your life with God. The core to your rope is God, and it is made of three strands, Father, Son, and Holy Spirit, so snugly twisted they exist as one, as your unbreakable God who is the source of your strength.

The sheath to your rope is made of three parts—body, mind, and spirit—carefully braided together into your one being. The combination of your sheath and your core is sublime. How profound to realize that each of us is a unique human being intimately connected with God, who lives within us and through us.

The kernmantle analogy offers more. Your core is strong enough to carry you to heaven (or to however you conceive of life after death) even if your sheath is unhealthy. Fraying and thinning of the braided sheath can occur because of unexplained illness, accidents, and trauma or because of poor maintenance—for example, unhealthy habits, chronic stress, and lack of attention to your emotional and spiritual health. Throughout this book I've talked about steps each of us can take to bring healing to our sheath, that is, to our mind, body, and spirit, regardless of the cause of the unhealthiness. When you cherish your mind, body, and spirit fibers in these ways, you will be better able to give full glory to God with your life. You will also feel better and suffer less.

Choice

You have to choose. This gift of God and fullness of health will not be there for you unless you accept it and commit to caring for your rope. You don't know how long your rope is, but just keep holding on. As long as you are alive, you have some ability to make choices about your rope—choices that can make it healthier. Even if you are terminally ill, you can still choose to love, forgive, and accept the will of God, which will help you to suffer far less than if you choose to be angry and blaming in your final days. Whether this reduction in suffering comes from God's healing touch or from the health benefits of reduced stress, I do not know. Either way, it is part of God's plan. You can make these choices about your rope right until the moment your life on Earth ends and you fall into the loving arms of our Lord and Savior.

A special feature of our braided sheath is that steps we take to heal one part of our sheath will ease the stress on the other two parts and promote healing of the whole sheath. This means you can start your healing process anywhere you are called to start, such as giving more time to God in prayer, starting a daily walking program, improving your diet, or joining a Bible study group. The healing processes merge just like the braided fibers merge. A great example is the well-known ability of exercise to improve mental health. This might lead to clarity and a deeper prayer life.

Remember Andrew. For him, the process started with an exercise boot camp to lose weight, but then led to many life changes. Now, several years later, he continues to thrive as he cares for himself, his family, and his church. For Liz, in my Serenity and Health group, Centering Prayer was key to dealing with stress and anxiety. Maybe you put too much junk food into your temple and are being called to eat more healthy foods. Coach Tate followed a biblical approach to eating, lost 200 pounds, and changed his whole life.[67]

---

67. https://www.serenityandhealth.com/meet-the-coach

As for myself, the first step I chose was to add prayer and then later swimming. What about you? Maybe you haven't committed to quiet prayer time every single day. Perhaps you need professional help for your anxiety or depression. We are all different. You know yourself. Choose a small step and move ahead. Get help if you are stuck.

As you take steps to work on your sheath, always trust in the absolute presence and strength of your core.

The above stories are examples of a positive cycle—when a positive step facilitates other positive steps that work together to enhance growth and healing. It's also possible to take steps that lead to a negative cycle. The more fibers on the sheath that are damaged, the more the surrounding parts are stressed and potentially damaged. That's what happened to Jim. Lack of exercise and outside interests resulted in more TV time, more snacking in the evening, weight gain, eventually knee pain aggravated by obesity, and finally a diagnosis of diabetes. He was depressed and felt far from God. All our lives are marked by ups and downs, positive and negative cycles. It is always within our power to change the direction—it starts with one step.

Beyond

As Christians, we believe we are part of the body of Christ, all of us connected in this one body. The positive steps we take will have ripple effects on our families, neighbors, and even strangers—because we are all connected. Prayer, a smile, a kind word, or a loving act make the body of Christ better as a whole, but any of these also reach every living human.

The connectedness extends beyond human beings to the entire natural world. St. Francis wrote eloquently about our Brother Sun and Sister Moon in his Canticle to the Sun.

Most of us have experienced the divine presence in natural creations of our world, whether it be a puppy, a mountain, the sea, or the stars and moon in the sky. Physicists observe the connections between elementary particles like quarks and the universe that is larger than we can even imagine.

How much influence does each of us have beyond ourselves? The answer is more than we can probably fathom.

Mystery

We cannot comprehend God, nor can we really understand how we have been saved by the death and resurrection of Jesus. This is mystery. Study, prayer, reading the Bible, and our reason will help us understand, but regardless of our efforts, belief comes down to a personal decision. Have you decided, yes or no, to accept the gift of faith and to believe? I decided yes.

The process of writing this book made me even more certain of my decision, while at the same time making me much more comfortable with the glorious mystery of it all. I'm better able to savor the present moment and let go of all I don't understand. I trust that Jesus values my well-intentioned efforts to do his will, even when I am confused.

Keys for You

Hold close the meanings of *mystery, oneness, steps,* and *trust.* Never forget the value of *silence, listening,* and *smiles.* Use the keys to physical health —*moving, walking, sleeping,* and *eating at least five servings of fruits and vegetables each day.*

You are free to *choose*—to believe in God and serve our Lord and Savior and to cherish your temple and do the best you can to care for it—or not to do those things. You made an important choice by reading this book and already may have tried some new and different steps. If you continue to be stressed, hurting, or anxious and do not know what to do next, please see Appendix I, "What's Next for You?" for help.

Last Words

My life has taught me the value of supplementing the rich practices of my Christian faith with healthy living, an embrace of each moment, and attention to my emotional health. As a result, I have learned how to better love God, myself, and others.

With a growing faith and trust in Jesus, I now rejoice to see how all these pieces fit together to create abundant health for me—and I want that for you as well. I am thrilled to share my story because I believe it can help you find your own path to better health of body, mind, and spirit. Let today be the day you choose to move forward on that path, starting with one small step. I know you can do it because you will have God at your side.

Appendices

Appendix I.

What's Next For You?

Be certain you understand the difference between your goals and your plans. Your goal is your long-term objective. Your plan, often called your action plan, describes the steps you will take to reach your goal. Your goal might be to reduce your stress and irritability; to be closer to God; to lose twenty pounds; or to run a marathon by the end of next year. You must prayerfully reflect as you decide on your goals, trying to discern God's will for you. Envision how you will feel when you reach your goal and hang on to that good feeling.

Then, sit down with a notebook and write down specific steps you can take to start moving toward your selected goal. This is your action plan, and, to make it work you must choose a first step that is small, very specific, and something you feel pretty confident you can accomplish and fit into your existing routine. Obviously, the details of your plan will depend on your personal goals and circumstances. Examples might be walking for 15 minutes after dinner twice a week or each Saturday for thirty minutes; setting the alarm ten minutes earlier five days a week for prayer or scripture reading; or, eliminating soda except for special occasions, at most once a week. You must hold yourself accountable by reviewing your progress weekly. It feels good to succeed with a plan, even if it is a small step. This confidence boost will empower you to continue and even advance your plan. If you didn't succeed, learn from that and start again, continuing to prayerfully reevaluate your progress at least once a week. I encourage you to use this weekly reflection on your action plan as part of your Sabbath routine.

If, however, you are too overwhelmed to even think of making an action plan, consider the following options.

- *Your Path*[68] is a four-week Serenity and Health online program I have made available to you. It is a self-help, go-at-your-own pace guide. Take your time, be patient with yourself and feel free to contact me for questions at dc@serenityandhealth.com.

- Alternatively, just follow these specific guidelines and trust God to be there with you:

  1. Start by adding fifteen minutes of prayer time each morning. Choose any kind of prayer that you like.

  2. If you still feel stuck after praying regularly for a while, start going for a ten- or twenty-minute walk (or some other physical activity if you have limitations) five or six times a week while you wait for clarity. You might get guidance as a word or insight from God, scripture, a neighbor, a Facebook post, or like Liz, from an announcement in your church bulletin.

---

68. To access the Your Path self-help program, go to https://www.serenityandhealth.com/yourpath

3. Finally, if you don't hear an answer, don't stop
    the daily prayer and regular exercise, but add
    something new to your routine, such as: jour-
    naling; a new prayer practice such as Center-
    ing Prayer; Bible study; joining a prayer group
    or other community that is meaningful to
    you; volunteering; participating in an exercise
    group; taking music lessons; reading a self-help
    book or any of the books I've referenced; or
    seeking professional help. I'm confident that, in
    God's time, an answer will come—maybe not
    a full solution, but an answer that will give you
    direction, relief, and hope.

- You also can subscribe to my monthly newsletter
  or follow me on Facebook.[69] I cover assorted topics
  related to health of body, mind, and spirit in my blog,
  Pop-Up Conversations, and other features. For Facebook followers, look for live sessions I will schedule
  during the first year after the book is published.

- Consider self-study. Here is a list of the books and
  links I found most helpful on my journey, along
  with my brief comments.

Mind/Body Psychology

Minding the Body, Mending the Mind by Joan Borysenko.
A classic by a pioneer of mind-body medicine.

---

69. To subscribe to the Serenity and Health newsletter and blog, go to https://www.
serenityandhealth.com/subscribe. Follow on Facebook @serenityandhealthdc
Follow on Twitter @donna chacko

Mind Over Mood: Change How You Feel by Changing the Way You Think by Dennis Greenberger and Christine A. Padesky. A practical book with guidelines and suggestions to help you grow from negative ways of thinking.

Full Catastrophe Living: Using the Wisdom of Your Body and Mind to Face Stress, Pain, and Illness (2nd ed), by Jon Kabat-Zinn. A comprehensive presentation by the founder of modern mindfulness/stress reduction.

The Road Less Traveled: A New Psychology of Love, Traditional Values, and Spiritual Growth, by M. Scott Peck. An old book packed with wisdom for our times. This book, along with *Sacrament of the Present Moment* (listed below), and *The Prophet* by Kahlil Gibran are the only books I have read multiple times in my life—and that speaks volumes!

The Body Keeps the Score: Brain, Mind, and Body in the Healing of Trauma by Bessel A. van der Kolk. A psychiatrist shares what he has learned about trauma and stress, the way they imprint in the body, and how the damage can be healed.

The Emotionally Healthy Woman by Geri Scazzero. The author is the wife of Pastor Peter Scazzero who wrote *Emotionally Health Spirituality*, listed below. These two books will greatly benefit anyone struggling in a relationship—these books offer a faith-based path to a better way.

Spiritual

Sacrament of the Present Moment by Jean-Pierre de Caussade (new translation by Kitty Muggeridge). A slim treasure written in the 1700s by a Jesuit priest, best prayed rather than read; transformational for me.

Devotional Classics, Selected Readings for Individuals and Groups by Richard J. Foster and James B. Smith. This book offers so much wisdom.

Intimacy With God: Introduction to Centering Prayer by Thomas Keating. In this book and the one below, Father Keating explores contemplative prayer and the psychology and spirituality of the true self/false self.

Open Mind, Open Heart (2nd ed.) by Thomas Keating.

Emotionally Healthy Spirituality by Peter Scazzero. I highly recommend this book, which I discuss in the first Serenity and Health Book Share blog post of August 8, 2019.

The Gift of Being Yourself, the Sacred Call to Self-Discovery by David G. Benner. 104 pages of wisdom about knowing God and knowing self.

Lifestyle Medicine

Disease-Proof: The Remarkable Truth About What Makes Us Well by David L. Katz. A doctor writes about eating and health.

Eat, Drink, and Be Healthy by Walter C. Willet. A comprehensive and readable guide to healthy eating.

Younger Next Year: Live Strong, Fit, and Sexy—Until You're 80 and Beyond by Chris Crowley and Henry S. Lodge. This book strongly emphasizes exercise and includes readable explanations about exercise physiology and the health benefits of exercise.

Websites and More

Contemplative Outreach at contemplativeoutreach.org provides a wealth of information about Contemplative Prayer.

Center for Action and Contemplation at cac.org is Father Richard Rohr's site. Learn more about the wisdom of the Christian contemplative tradition and its emergence in service to the healing of our world.

Healthy Eating, Harvard School of Public Health at https://www.hsph.harvard.edu/nutritionsource/healthy-eating-plate/ provides detailed guidance, in a simple format, to help you make the best eating choices.

Physical Fitness: A Pathway to Health and Resilience. To download this excellent 2013 summary go to Self-Study Resources at serenityandhealth.com and click the link found at the bottom of the page.

Information and advice about exercise:

https://www.danielplan.com/fitness/
https://www.sparkpeople.com/resource/fitness.asp
https://www.cdc.gov/physicalactivity/index.html

Appendix II.

Centering Prayer

Centering Prayer is a receptive method of Christian silent prayer that prepares us to receive the gift of contemplative prayer, prayer in which we experience God's presence within us, closer than breathing, closer than thinking, closer than consciousness itself.

GUIDELINES FOR CENTERING PRAYER

- Choose a sacred word as the symbol of your intention to consent to God's presence and action within.

- Sitting comfortably and with eyes closed, settle briefly and silently introduce the sacred word as the symbol of your consent to God's presence and action within.

- When engaged with your thoughts, return ever so gently to the sacred word.

- At the end of the prayer period, remain in silence with eyes closed for a couple of minutes.

Copied with permission from ContemplativeOutreach.org

———•———

Thomas Keating states the sacred word is not a mantra, more of an anchor. He asserts that the hardest part of Centering Prayer is actually just sitting down to do it—making the decision and then doing it. That certainly has been my experience. The above-mentioned website is a wonderful resource to learn more about Centering Prayer.

Appendix III.

Favorite Prayers

Memorare

Remember, O most gracious Virgin Mary, that never was it known that anyone who fled to thy protection, implored thy help, or sought thine intercession was left unaided.

Inspired by this confidence, I fly unto thee, O Virgin of virgins, my mother; to thee do I come, before thee I stand, sinful and sorrowful. O Mother of the Word Incarnate, despise not my petitions, but in thy mercy hear and answer me.

Amen.

———•———

Serenity Prayer,

God, grant me the serenity to accept the things
I cannot change,
the courage to change the things I can, and
the wisdom to know the difference.

———•———

Serenity Prayer
(long version)

God, give me grace to accept with serenity
the things that cannot be changed,
Courage to change the things
which should be changed,
and the Wisdom to distinguish
the one from the other.
Living one day at a time,
Enjoying one moment at a time,
Accepting hardship as a pathway to peace,
Taking, as Jesus did,
This sinful world as it is,
Not as I would have it,
Trusting that You will make all things right,
If I surrender to Your will,
So that I may be reasonably happy in this life,
And supremely happy with You forever in the
next.
Amen.

—Reinhold Niebuhr

———•—•———

Modified Serenity Prayer
(source unknown)

God, grant me the serenity to accept the people I
cannot change, the courage to change the one I can,
and the wisdom to know that one is me. Amen.

———•—•———

Thomas Merton's prayer, from his book
Thoughts in Solitude

"My Lord God, I have no idea where I am going. I do not see the road ahead of me. I cannot know for certain where it will end. Nor do I really know myself, and the fact that I think that I am following your will does not mean that I am actually doing so. But I believe that the desire to please you does in fact please you. And I hope I have that desire in all that I am doing. I hope that I will never do anything apart from that desire. And I know that if I do this you will lead me by the right road, though I may know nothing about it. Therefore will I trust you always, though I may seem to be lost and in the shadow of death. I will not fear, for you are ever with me, and you will never leave me to face my perils alone."

Donna's morning prayers, her
modifications of classics and originals

O my God, I offer you this day, bless it and accept it for thy greater honor and glory. I offer you every thought, word, deed, demeanor, action, attitude, posture, smile, and my attempts to be gentle, humble, and to listen. I offer you my aches, pains, aging, and wrinkles. I offer you my time, lists, goals, and intentions. I surrender all to you. Amen.

Modified Suscipe Prayer

Take my freedom, my memory, my understanding, and my will. All that I have and cherish you have given me. I surrender it all to be governed by your holy will. Amen.

———•·———

Modified Prayer of St. Francis

Lord, make me an instrument of your peace. Where there is hatred, let me sow love; injury, pardon; doubt, faith; despair, hope; darkness, light; sickness, healing; monkey mind, peace of Christ.

Where there is injustice, prejudice, judgment, selfishness, jealousy, and pride—may there be justice, respect, a reverent kind of love for every living being, selfless generosity, joy, and happiness for all the good things that other people do and have, and a warm, gentle humility.

Where there is pain or any cross to carry, may I carry it like a beautiful large bouquet of flowers, holding it to my heart and then raising it to God, for His honor and glory, the salvation of souls, forgiveness of sins, and healing as He sees fit.

Where there is worry, fear, anxiety, or stress, may there be absolute trust in You, our Lord and our God.

Divine Master, grant that I may seek not so much to be understood as to understand, to be consoled as to console, to be loved as to love, and to be listened to as to listen. For it is in giving that we receive, pardoning that we are pardoned, and dying that we are born to eternal life. Amen.

——•——

My Lord, Let my hands be your hands, my heart be your heart, may I see as you see and, above all, listen as you listen.

——•——

May I Stand up tall, Smile and Listen!!

——•——

Prayer for Our Parish

Dear God,

We of St. Marks come humbly before you, praying together to tell you how much we love you and need you.

We are forever grateful to you for your mercy, for our faith, and for all our blessings. We especially pray for wisdom, trust, and courage to help us be better instruments of your love. Help each of us, O God, to be open to your will so that we may better serve you as stewards of your gifts and talents. Help us to show love, generosity, and friendship to those who are different from us and to those in need.

Thank you for the many faithful of our parish. With your help we will embrace our challenges as opportunities to grow closer to you as individuals and as a parish!

O Dear God, we make a joyful noise of praise and thanksgiving to you as we turn to you, trusting in the Holy Name of Jesus, who lives and reigns with you in the unity of the Holy Spirit, one God for ever and ever. Amen.

[This prayer was written by me in August 2013 for St. Mark the Evangelist Catholic Church and is regularly recited at daily Mass. Other churches are invited to use it as is or modify it in any way.]

Author's Note

In *Pilgrimage: A Doctor's Healing Journey* I used pseud-
onyms to describe all family members, friends, patients,
colleagues, and church members, except for a very few
individuals whom I identify with a full name, not just a first
name. All descriptions of patients and church members have
been changed to make them unidentifiable. Some descriptions of patients are composites. Any quotes from patients
or group participants came directly from a real person.

To write this book, I relied on my memory, my early
diaries, and a detailed journal I wrote during the illness
of my first husband. Having now completed this deeply
introspective project, I understand that the truths and
perceptions I have presented to you may be totally different
from those of other participants in the story.

I write from my perspective as a Christian, but I believe
my health message is valid for anyone who believes in a
higher power by any name. All scripture quotes are from
the New American Bible (Revised Edition). I use the mas-
culine when referring to God. When it comes to gender
pronouns, I tried to use he or she at random.

Acknowledgments

My ever-present champion during the six-and-a-half years I spent writing *Pilgrimage* was my dear husband. He was unflagging in his encouragement and never once expressed skepticism about the thousands of hours I spent hunched in my office in front of my computer. I love him very much and am so grateful for his good humor, his laugh, and what he has taught me about staying in the moment.

To my three daughters, I express my deepest gratitude for their encouragement, questions, and challenges as I was writing this book. I acknowledge the pain they must have felt by having the muck of our family life stirred up and brought to the surface, and I am sorry for this. They are brave and strong—I love them so much and am profoundly grateful to have them in my life.

I also want to thank Javier, my son-in-law, for his very patient tech support and assistance with the writing software Scrivener.

My two brothers and their wives were always supportive and available for ideas and fact checking. My twin's wife was particularly helpful with design input for the book cover and website.

Outside of family, the person most critical to the success of this book is Julie Epstein. As a media consultant (also friend and neighbor) she worked on my website, various programs, book editing, and marketing—always with incredible energy, skill, and initiative. I've thanked her a million times. It's a pleasure to be able to publicly acknowledge all her contributions and thank her one more time.

I also appreciate Desiree Magney and Emily Rich, instructors at my first (and only) writing class, "Finding Your Memoir Voice" at the Writer's Center in Bethesda, Maryland, in early 2018. They encouraged me and were the first ones to tell me, "Remember: show, not tell."

Similarly, I want to thank the Hyattsville (Maryland) Writers group, to whom I shared the early versions of book—especially Mark Goodson, Kimberly Schmidt, and Kristi Janzen—for their patience and suggestions.

I want to recognize Devra Torres and Peg O'Brien, my very first readers of an early version of the book. Peg has participated in multiple Serenity and Health programs and has constantly encouraged me. Also thanks to beta readers Margo Bellock, Lisa Bank-Williams, and Peggy Winton. I'm a lucky lady to have good friends like these—and many others who patiently listened to me as I sometimes droned on about my book.

Father Roberto Cortes is the pastor of my parish, St. Marks, in Hyattsville, Maryland. From the beginning he welcomed my Serenity and Health programs at church and encouraged my efforts to promote faith-based health. For this I am very grateful.

Other professionals who helped me get through this process are Father Thomas Frank, my spiritual director and reader of an early (atrocious) version of chapter 12 about my spiritual life, and Marilyn Williams, my therapist, who has been wonderfully supportive and reviewed chapter 11 about my emotional journey. How can I fully express my gratitude for help like this?

Over the years I worked with two wise editors, Martha Murphy and Margot Starbuck. They helped me shape the book into what it became. I was very green and greatly appreciated both their expertise and their gentle patience.

In the process of learning how to write and market a book, I reached out and talked with a large number of writers and other professionals who were unfailingly generous with their time and advice—including all who read and endorsed *Pilgrimage*. I want to express my gratitude to each of them, listed here in no particular order: Kenny Lin, Christine Sine, Chris Manion, Tonya Kubo, Christa Hutchins, Jem Sullivan, Mark Greiner, Harriet Michael, Kristen Brock, Amaryliss Sanchez, Marguerite Duane, Dale Fletcher, Elizabeth Guss, Ryan Atkins, Brian Plachta, Renee Catacolos, Mitch Daniels, Evelyn Sherwood, Doris Swift, Cory Carlson, Ted Ficken, Janelle Goetcheus, Susan Riggs, and those who endorsed my book too late for this list. To anyone I may have forgotten, I offer a special hug.

I am grateful to my friend and neighbor, Susanna Limon, who assumed the role of cheerleader through this process.

I also acknowledge those who spent their precious time working on my launch team, especially my team lead, Caryn Tilton, along with Margo Bellock and Peg O'Brien. I am very grateful and wish I could throw a big party for all of them today.

The birthing of the book was greatly aided by the expert coaching help of Chad R. Allen, a kind and wise man who has a knack of getting the best out of writers. I'm very grateful to Chad—he doesn't know it, but he's probably not seen the last of me.

Similarly, I want to acknowledge Erin Bartels for her copywriting/marketing assistance and her skill in telling the essence of a story in just a few words.

I'm thrilled to recognize the wonderful team of professionals at Luminare Press, publisher of *Pilgrimage*. I knew the first time I spoke with Patricia that her team was for me. So, to Patricia Marshall, Kim Harper-Kennedy, Jamie Passaro, Kristen Brack, and copyeditor Denise Szott, I voice my profound gratitude—for your professionalism, knowledge, and care as you worked with me to bring my book to life.

Finally, I offer gratitude to everyone who is included in this book in some form or fashion—by name, with a pseudonym, as part of a composite, or as an influencer. This includes a special prayer of gratitude for those who are no longer living, especially my parents and my first husband, father of my three daughters. I am deeply indebted.

Above all, I give glory and thanks to God, the primary driver of *Pilgrimage*.

Give thanks to the Lord for he is good,
his mercy endures forever!
Psalm 107:1

More About the Author

Daughter, sister, wife, doctor, mother, grandmother... in that order. It all started in Portland, Oregon, where Donna was born and raised, along with her twin brother and older brother.

After attending Catholic schools through high school, she went to college in Oregon, married, and moved with her husband to California for medical school at the University of California, Davis. After completing their professional training and having three daughters, they settled in St. Petersburg, Florida, where they raised their family and Donna practiced radiation oncology for nearly twenty years.

Donna's husband died in 1997. Three years later, at the age of fifty-one, she left radiation oncology to begin a three-year family medicine residency. Donna made this bold change because she wanted to be able to care for the poor as a primary care doctor.

After her training, with her children all out of the home, Donna moved to Washington, DC, where she worked in a community health center and at Christ House, a medical recovery facility for the homeless. She retired in 2013 and now lives in University Park, Maryland, with her second husband. In 2014 Donna founded her Serenity and Health ministry to promote health of body, mind, and spirit, starting with programs at her church.

Her favorite pastimes are reading, gardening, walking, staying connected to long-distance family, visiting with her women friends, and watching *Masterpiece Theater* and NBA games with her husband.